In Search of the Black Box

A Report on the Proceedings of a
Workshop on Micro-Climates Held at the
Royal Ontario Museum, February 1978

RŎM
Royal Ontario Museum
1979

©The Royal Ontario Museum, 1979
100 Queen's Park, Toronto, Ontario M5S 2C6

ISBN 0-88854-244-5

Printed and bound in Canada

Cover photo: Ptolemaic Egyptian, mummiform mask

Contents

Part III
Recommendations and Conclusions

Figures

Foreword

The publication of *In Search of the Black Box* marks the completion of the "definition" phase of environment planning for the future care of those collections which in every museum are especially designated as highly sensitive to climatic change. It describes the background, proceedings, and results of a workshop on micro-climates held at the Royal Ontario Museum (ROM), in February 1978, with the aim of arriving at that "definition".

Concern for, discussion of, and conferences on museum environments are not new in the Conservation world; however, we believe this workshop was unique in that its main purpose was to define the needs and establish the specifications from which we can move directly into the development of equipment.

The valuable recommendations derived from the workshop were possible only because of the combined experience, enthusiasm, and hard work of the participants, and I thank them most sincerely for that commitment. The participants were:

Joseph Di Profio, Assistant Director, Education and Communication, ROM; Chairman

Ian Hodkinson, Head, Conservation and Restoration Laboratory, National Gallery of Canada, Ottawa

Arthur Jones, Project Office, ROM (Engineering Interface, Ltd., Consultants)

Betty Kaser, Staff Consultant, ROM

William Maxwell, Convectron, Inc., Consulting Mechanical Engineers, New York

Kenneth Macleod, Chief, Environment
and Deterioration Research, Canadian
Conservation Institute, Ottawa

Gillian Moir, Conservator, ROM

Tim Moore, Supervisor, Exhibit Production
and Maintenance, Exhibit Design Services, ROM

Elizabeth Phillimore, Head, Conservation
Department, ROM

Lorne Render, Head, Exhibit Design Services,
ROM

George de W. Rogers, Conservation Division,
National Historic Parks and Sites, Ottawa

Mervyn Ruggles, Professor of Art Conservation,
Queen's University, Kingston

Henry Sears, Coordinator, ECTF, ROM
(Urban Design Consultants)

Stephen Stone, Convectron, Inc., Consulting
Mechanical Engineers, New York

LeMar Terry, Lighting Consultant, Metropolitan
Museum of Art, New York

Philip Ward, Director of Conservation Services,
Canadian Conservation Institute, Ottawa

I am grateful to the Director of the Royal Ontario Museum,
Dr. James E. Cruise, and to Joseph R. Di Profio, Assistant
Director for Education and Communication and at that time
also Chairman of the Exhibits Communication Task Force, for
their encouragement and foresight, and also for their gener-
ous sponsorship of the workshop.

My warm and special thanks are due here to Henry Sears of
Urban Design Consultants and his Assistant, Betty Kaser, for
their seemingly tireless enthusiasm and creativity throughout
all phases of planning and execution.

Last, but far from least my appreciation to Gillian Moir for her assistance in drafting this document from her meticulous notes of the proceedings and for providing, throughout the writing, a calm sense of balance which was invaluable.

Elizabeth A. Phillimore
Head, Conservation Department
Royal Ontario Museum
March 1, 1979

Part I
Background to the Workshop

Part I
Background to the
Workshop

A. The ROM Planning Process

The Royal Ontario Museum is at present undergoing an extensive programme of renovation and new construction necessary to relieve the pressure of its growing collections and activities. The planning process began in 1970 with an expansion feasibility study. The goals of the Museum as a whole, as an administrative unit, and as a physical structure were carefully explored through questionnaires and surveys involving staff members on all levels, outside experts, members of the local community, and Museum visitors. The first document produced by this process was the *Guidelines for Planning* report, issued in April, 1975. It contained a statement which emphasized the need for the types of solutions discussed by the workshop participants three years later:

> A first and fundamental obligation of any
> museum must surely be to preserve the unique
> and priceless objects in its care against
> deterioration. Some of the processes of
> deterioration are rapid, some are slow. But
> a museum must look to all posterity, since a
> high proportion of the objects in its care
> can never be replaced.

The *ROM Statement of Intent*, issued in September, 1975, confirmed this concern:

> All feasible steps should be taken during
> physical planning, to correct the present
> uncontrolled environmental conditions within
> the existing structures, which threaten the
> well-being of the collections.

On September 23, 1975, a meeting was held to establish basic

internal environmental requirements for the ROM, as an
essential basis for preliminary design investigations.
The meeting was attended by the ROM Director, the then Head
of the Conservation Department, the architects, and the
mechanical and electrical engineering consultants (Mathers
& Haldenby/Moffat Moffat & Kinoshita, associated architects
Engineering Interface Ltd., mechanical engineering consultants, Ellard-Willson Ltd., electrical engineering consultants). The memorandum requesting attendance at the meeting said, in part:

> We are working with existing buildings
> not designed for close environmental
> control, and the achievement of year-
> round standards with very close tolerances
> may well be impossible, and will certainly
> be very costly. It is important, then, that
> we establish realistic base requirements
> which give the designers as much latitude
> as possible consistent with good conserva-
> torial practice. This may mean the estab-
> lishment of general conditions with fairly
> wide tolerances acceptable for most collect-
> ions, and the establishment of special "micro-
> climate" requirements for particularly vulner-
> able collections.

The Exhibits Communication Task Force (ECTF) was established
in September, 1976 to ensure that the policies and procedures
which are to guide the ROM in the development of galleries
and exhibitions reflect a wide body of opinions within the
Museum. The evolution of those policies involved considerable interaction with virtually all departments of the
Museum as well as with many interested individuals. One of
the issues identified in this process was the need to exam-
ine the most effective means of producing micro-climates,
and a workshop was proposed.

Opportunities and Constraints, the first report of the ECTF,
completed on September 1, 1977, emphasized the problems of
conditions within the existing building, and noted that
"the result is that there has been considerable deterioration of artifacts over the years". It recommended as policy,
"that consultation with the Conservation Department be a
mandatory procedure in the process of developing galleries".
It also noted that "the Conservation Department should define
the appropriate conditions for preserving artifacts". The
workshop was initiated to explore how to create those conditions.

B. The Collections of the ROM

The artifacts which form the ROM collections are extremely varied in nature, material, shape, size, and response to environment. The following table shows the great variety of problem materials held by each department.

DEPARTMENT	APPROX. NO. OF ITEMS IN COLLECTION	PROBLEM MATERIALS
ART AND ARCHAEOLOGY DEPARTMENTS		
Ethnology		
Native peoples of Canada, American southwest, Mexico, Central and South America, Africa, Indonesia, South Pacific, and Australia	36,000	bone, ivory, porcupine quills, hair, fur, feathers, wood, bark, tapa, straw, reeds, grass, root
New World Archaeology		
Ontario history and pre-history; Central and South American archaeology	763,000	bone, teeth
European		
Applied arts of western Europe from the mediaeval period to the early 20th century; philately	50,000	leather, gilt and inlaid furniture, polychrome sculpture, rare books, illuminated manuscripts, musical instruments, ivory, horn, tortoise-shell, miniature paintings

DEPARTMENT	APPROX. NO. OF ITEMS IN COLLECTION	PROBLEM MATERIALS
Textiles		
Costumes, accessories, and textiles from all cultures, including rugs and tapestries	100,000	Coptic and Tiraz fragments; rugs; feathers; metal hooks, buttons, beads, etc.; furs
Greek and Roman		
European pre-history; Aegean Bronze Age and Cyprus; Greek historical periods, including western Asia Minor; Roman Italy and provinces; Anglo-Saxon, Viking, and Merovingian Europe	49,000	marble and limestone, bronze, glass, encaustic paintings
Egyptian		
pre-history; Pre-Dynastic; Archaic; Old, Middle, and New Kingdoms; Nubia, Egyptians abroad	10,000	mummies and mummy cases, cartonnage masks, papyrus, leather, bronze
West Asian		
late prehistoric Near East, Mesopotamia, Syro-Palestine, Islamic cultures	22,000	bronze, painted stucco, ivory, illuminated books, Persian miniatures, lacquered wood
Far Eastern		
early Chinese Bronze Age; Buddhist arts; pictorial and decorative arts of China, Japan, Korea, India, and southeast Asia	100,000	Japanese screens, lacquer, Chinese bronzes, Japanese swords
Canadiana		
artifacts and pictures of Canadian origin or context	10,000	oil paintings, watercolours and other works on paper, furniture, treen

DEPARTMENT	APPROX. NO. OF ITEMS IN COLLECTION	PROBLEM MATERIALS
SCIENCE DEPARTMENTS		
Invertebrate Palaeontology		
invertebrate fossils	100,000	none
Vertebrate Palaeontology		
vertebrate fossils and skeletons	40,000	bones
Ichthyology and Herpetology		
Canadian and deep sea fish, world reptiles and amphibians	42,000	aquaria
Mammalogy		
Ontario, neotropic and African mammals; endangered species; bats	78,000	mounted specimens; skin and fur; paintings; watercolours and other works of art on paper
Mineralogy and Geology		
specimens and gems	155,000	some minerals for frailty and dust
Botany and Palaeobotany		
mostly dried herbarium materials	300,000	none
Ornithology		
world-wide birds	130,000	feathers, skin and bones; some mounted specimens; paintings; watercolours and other works of art on paper

DEPARTMENT	APPROX. NO. OF ITEMS IN COLLECTION	PROBLEM MATERIALS
Entomology arthropods; insects, arachnids; centipedes and millipedes	1,000,000	mounted specimens for frailty and dust
Invertebrate Zoology crustaceans, molluscs, sponges	7,000	none

C. The ROM before Expansion

The ROM is located at the southwest corner of Queen's Park and Bloor Street West in central Toronto. It is well served by public transportation with the Museum subway station almost at its doorstep. It is adjacent to the University of Toronto and was a part of the University until it became independent in 1968.

The original building - the west block - was started in 1910 and opened in 1914. The remainder of the H-shaped main building was built in 1932. The Planetarium, Exhibition Hall, and the cafeteria were later additions.

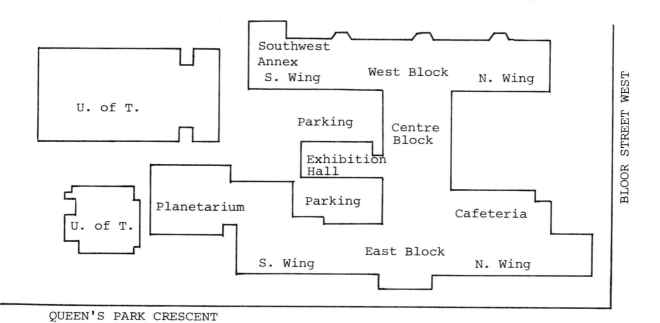

Figure 1:   The existing ROM building.

As the plan above indicates, two University of Toronto buildings are immediately adjacent to the Museum building, south of the Planetarium and of the west block. These effectively prevent any future expansion to the south.

The west block is constructed of load-bearing masonry walls. The east and central blocks are of steel construction with masonry non-bearing walls. All of these blocks are heated by steam with the piping chased into the masonry walls. The heating system is antiquated, and the water and drainage piping have seriously deteriorated. The power supply is inadequate, and air climate control is limited to the Planetarium and one of the existing galleries.

D. The Expansion Plan

The expansion plan consists of three basic stages - the demolition of some of the existing structures (see figure 2), the addition of two new buildings - the Curatorial Centre and the Terrace Galleries (see figure 3), and the renovation of the west, centre, and east blocks.

Figure 2 indicates those existing structures which are to be demolished. The demolition of Exhibition Hall and the Planetarium annex have already taken place, the excavation for the new curatorial centre completed, and construction begun.

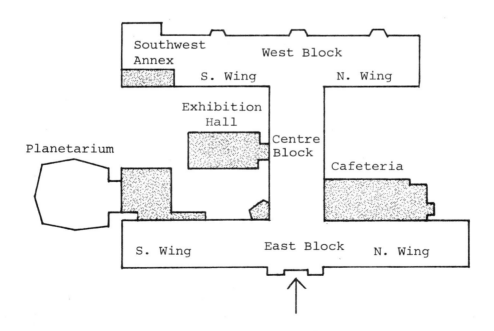

Figure 2:   Existing structures to be demolished.

Figure 3 shows new structures to be added and indicates the
terminology which has been adopted for the various parts of
existing and future buildings and their surroundings.

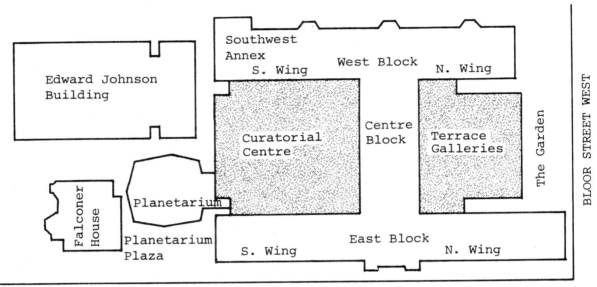

Figure 3:   Proposed new structures.

The basic approach which has been developed for use of the
site includes retention of the older buildings which have
been designated as historic structures, infilling the court-
yards to the north and south of the buildings with new structures, and preservation of some of the parkland to the north.

The south courtyard will be replaced by a self-contained
curatorial office and reference collection centre of nine
floors, of which three floors will be below grade. This
Curatorial Centre will be devoted to offices, laboratories,
workrooms, and the library, with 30% of the space taken up
by reference and rotating display collections in partially
compacted storage.

The new structure to the north, the Terrace Galleries, is to
be six storeys of which two storeys are below grade. This
will mainly contain new gallery spaces of approximately
5379.3 m^2 (59,770 sq. ft.). Immediately to the north of
this building will be landscaped parkland accessible to the
public. The Museum's Ming tomb, with its massive archways
and guardian figures, which currently stands in a garden setting in the existing north courtyard, will be relocated to
the main floor level of the Terrace Galleries in a special

gallery of its own, and will be visible from the new park and from the street beyond.

The new structures - the Curatorial Centre and the Terrace Galleries - will be separated from the old exterior walls by multi-storey skylit atrium spaces. These atrium spaces deal with the problem of various and complex level differences between existing and new construction, provide room for visitor circulation, introduce diffused natural light, and act as a visual transition and orientation space. The existing exterior walls can thus be preserved intact, and their rich and handsome facades will enhance the appearance of the new galleries.

Most of the existing building will be returned to its original function as public galleries. These have been significantly reduced in area over the years by the growing demands for offices, activity areas, and storage spaces for reference and rotating display collections. The present wings will be completely renovated, a process which will include cleaning and restoring the original exterior walls, blocking in most of the existing windows, installing ultraviolet filtering glass in windows which will remain, and adding insulated interior plaster walls for increased energy savings. Complete new mechanical and electrical services will be installed, including new plumbing and drainage systems, a fire protection sprinkler system, improved power supply and wiring, and most importantly, a modern heating, ventilating, and air-conditioning system.

A new Exhibition Hall for temporary exhibitions, with special climate controls, will be established on the first floor of the existing southeast wing.

Part II
The Workshop

Part II
The Workshop

A. The Scope of the Workshop

The purpose of this workshop was to explore practical ways
of producing micro-climates for displaying museum materials
which cannot withstand exposure to fluctuations of ambient
gallery conditions. Existing solutions to the problems of
creating and sustaining micro-climates have included docu-
mented pieces of research and some successful but very spe-
cialized applications. In the hope of consolidating the
existing information into a more coherent whole and possibly
discovering new solutions, it was decided to hold this workshop. The aim was to assemble experienced people in all of
the fields involved - conservation, design, and mechanical
engineering; analyse the present state of the art; and determine whether there might be viable new ways to approach
the problem. This was to be the first time the field of
micro-climates would be discussed in such a concentrated
study by a group which was expert on all facets of the problem. The emphasis was to be on the production of practical
solutions, not merely the exploration of abstract ideas.

The workshop explored a variety of questions throughout the
three days. Most generally these focused around the following main problem areas:

> - *Which artifacts do not require micro-*
>   *climates?*
>
> - *Which artifacts need micro-climates which*
>   *can be provided using existing solutions?*
>
> - *Which artifacts require new solutions?*
>
> - *What are appropriate solutions to the problems*
>   *of case design?*

- *Which buffers are appropriate?*

- *Which mechanical solutions are appropriate?*

- *What are the requirements for new mechanical solutions, including product parameters?*

The workshop covered four main areas of discussion:

- the physical and environmental conditions in the present ROM building, and those proposed for the expanded and renovated museum;

- sensitivities of museum artifacts to temperature, relative humidity, light, dust, and pollution;

- the form of display units, such as cases and period names, which are to enclose micro-climates. These were examined with respect to the needs of the artifacts from the viewpoint of designers, curators, and conservators;

- the nature and use of micro-climates themselves. These were discussed in terms of energy saving, the appropriateness of their use to the ROM's collections and environmental conditions, the advisability of using sealed or "leaking" cases, construction materials, and lighting methods.

B. Preparation for the Workshop

In order to help make the workshop effective and productive, the Conservation Department, with assistance from the Exhibit Design Services Department and the ECTF, provided a considerable collection of material in advance. Participants in the workshop were told:

> The purpose of this workshop is to develop practical ways of producing micro-climates for displaying the material which cannot stand exposure to the fluctuations of ambient gallery conditions. It is hoped that this will be accomplished by group discussions drawing on the expertise of all workshop participants. This information package is designed not only to provide you with the material pertinent to this problem but also to provide an insight into the consultative nature of the ROM's planning process to date.

The advance information package contained the following:

- a description of the ROM collections indicating the nature of the collections by departments, with some indication of the number of items in each collection, and particular material in each collection which was likely to be a source of conservation concern.

- a categorization of sensitivity of museum artifacts to temperature, relative humidity, light, and dust.

- a description of the ambient gallery conditions as they exist in the current buildings and as they are planned in the proposed expanded Museum.

- an indication of the display considerations for micro-climates. This included a list of likely space modules and some of the construction issues which must be explored.

- a compilation of selected available information on existing solutions to micro-climates.

In addition to these documents developed especially for the workshop, other documents were provided for the participants. These included the following:

- excerpts from the *Final Planning Report*, Volume 1, (November 1977, Royal Ontario Museum), dealing with mechanical and electrical systems and environmental controls to be provided within the Museum.

- a bulletin of the Exhibits Communication Task Force dated November 1977 on Gallery Planning.

- regulations for the internal display and handling of artifacts at the ROM as developed by the Conservation Department.

- excerpts from the Engineering Interface Report on Environmental Conditions for the ROM dated November 3, 1976.

A separately bound report of the ECTF - *Opportunities and Constraints*, (November 1977, ROM) was also included for the information of the participants.

Participants were also given an agenda which indicated the main issues to be discussed throughout the workshop and a series of questions which were to be raised and dealt with specifically at varying stages of the deliberations.

C. General Environmental Conditions within the ROM

The conservation of artifacts in a museum begins with the quality of the general environmental conditions available. The first working session of the workshop was devoted to a presentation of the ambient conditions proposed for the ROM and a description of the systems which would make these conditions available. This presentation was made by Arthur Jones, of Engineering Interface Ltd., the engineers responsible for design of the mechanical systems for the new and renovated buildings. These systems are described in Appendix A.

This workshop provided the first opportunity for a detailed discussion of the conservation implications of the mechanical system and wall structures. Although discussions had taken place prior to this time, the exchanges that took place during the sessions stimulated some important new insights, resulting in changes to the design of the building and the mechanical systems.

1. DESCRIPTION OF THE ENVIRONMENTAL CONDITIONS

Two important provisions required of the architects and engineers were environmental protection for the artifacts and a comfortable climate for Museum visitors and staff. In the old building, heated by steam radiators, the relative humidity would plunge to winter lows of 5%, while in the summer, temperatures in galleries and offices would be in the 90° F range, and humidities would rise as high as 100%. Not only was this extremely uncomfortable for human beings, it was causing untold damage to artifacts as they contracted, expanded, warped, corroded, and in other ways reacted to these extreme changes. It was essential that the architects and engineers improve these conditions.

A major constraint was the construction of the existing building. If stone and masonry walls are exposed to a high interior humidity during the winter, moisture permeates the porous outer walls and freezes on contact with the cold outside air, expanding and causing the stone to break apart. It was suggested at an early stage of planning that the building be provided with a vapour barrier/insulation envelope which could contain a suitable, reasonably constant climate without damage to the structural fabric. This, however, proved far too expensive a solution and could only be used for small sections of the building, such as the new Exhibition Hall. It would be possible, though, through the use of modern air conditioning equipment, to improve the base climate greatly and to keep it at a relatively constant level during each season.

The system the engineers designed to maintain this new climate was responsive to a most demanding constraint - cost. In these days of fuel crisis and increasing inflation, a system was needed that would be both energy- and cost-efficient. The system that was decided upon used conventional mechanisms made more effective by the use of wall insulation, double-glazing, and ingenious recycling methods. Heat generated by lights, equipment, and people will be reclaimed by the air-conditioning systems and used in the heating of both the building and the hot water supply. Extra hot water heating for very cold days is expected to be needed for only 25 or 30 hours a year. There will also be provision for future solar collection and thermal water storage, when such systems become practical additions. It has been calculated that the new mechanical equipment will increase power consumption by 25% per square foot, but the recycling system will <u>decrease</u> heating energy use by 30% per square foot. The use of machines which turn themselves off when not needed will also result in energy savings which will write off their cost within two years of operation.

When the ROM's new environmental systems were first being designed, the plan had been to provide a base climate with a relative humidity (RH) range of 25% (winter minimum) to 50% (summer maximum) in the renovated north and south wings of the existing building. A "prime climate" with a relative humidity range of 35% to 50% was then planned for both parts of the new construction, the Curatorial Centre and Terrace Galleries, as well as the existing Centre Block which joined them. These areas would then have been suitable for artifacts which require higher and more stable relative humidities.

As the design evolved, however, it became evident that this prime climate would be impossible to achieve in the Centre Block because of the roof construction. The revised design limited the prime climate to new construction only - the Curatorial Centre and the Terrace Galleries. During the workshop it was revealed that the design had changed again and that the Terrace Galleries were to have the same ambient conditions as the existing building - i.e., a relative humidity range of 25% to 50%. The new walls, like the old ones, would not be of a standard able to accommodate a high degree of humidity in the winter time.

The need for energy conservation and the constraints imposed by the existing masonry structure dictated the limits and range of environmental conditions that could be produced. An annual temperature range throughout the museum of 21° to 23.5°C (70° to 76°F) was established, with 23.5°C (76°F) being the maximum summer temperature. It was determined that the relative humidity levels would necessarily range from a 25% winter minimum to a 50% summer maximum with a daily allowable variation of 10%RH. These variations are rather large from a conservation point of view, but it was felt that more stringent controls were too expensive or, in some cases, physically impossible to achieve. Air will be filtered of particulate contaminants to 10 microns in size with 99% efficiency, and to 1 micron with 90 to 95% efficiency; gaseous contaminants such as sulphur dioxide, ozone, and nitrous oxides will also be removed.

The Curatorial Centre will have a more desirable yearly humidity range of 35% to 50%, with a daily maximum variation of 6%RH. The reason that this prime space is given over to support functions rather than to galleries, is that sensitive artifacts can only be displayed for relatively short periods if rapid deterioration is to be prevented. Because these artifacts must spend much of their lives in storage, it is the storage areas that need optimum conditions. Included with this rotating material are the reference collections which are worked with daily by curators and researchers. Laboratories also need the more sophisticated environmental support systems able to be provided in the Curatorial Centre. Special climates will be provided within the Curatorial Centre storage areas where artifacts require cooler, drier, or moister conditions. These conditions can only be duplicated in the galleries through the use of micro-climates.

The system designed to provide the ROM's new environment is a sophisticated, energy- and cost-efficient system. The baseline standards it can achieve are suitable for about 90% of the Museum's artifacts. It is the remaining 10% of materials that demand special conditions and which will have to be protected by micro-climates. In this manner mixed collections can be displayed together in one gallery, and there is a greater energy saving in providing special micro-climates only for the 10% of the collections that need them.

2.   ISSUES ARISING FROM THE ENVIRONMENTAL CONDITIONS

a) THE TERRACE GALLERIES

Several months prior to the workshop, the ECTF understood that the newly constructed Terrace Galleries would be able to provide a base climate with a relative humidity range of 35% to 51% and that the galleries in the old building could only be improved to a range of 25% to 50%. This implied that moderately sensitive artifacts, where possible, would most logically be housed in the new Terrace Galleries even though this would place a major constraint on overall gallery planning. (Extremely sensitive artifacts would still require micro-climates.) In order to maintain these two different climates, an air-lock separation would be needed between the Terrace Galleries and the Centre Block. However, an air-lock system large enough to handle a class of 40 students would consume a substantial amount of gallery space, further constraining gallery planning. Moreover it was also felt that the double set of air-lock doors would creat a psychological barrier to visitors to the galleries beyond.

The ECTF had concluded that an air-lock at the entrance to the Terrace Galleries was not a satisfactory solution, and that the only logical choice was to isolate the artifacts within the gallery in one large, or a series of smaller, environmentally controlled cases. Once this conclusion was reached, it became obvious that the base climate being supplied in the Terrace Galleries could be allowed to match the Centre Block (25%-50%), and they would not need to be separated. There would therefore be a saving in space and energy.

The workshop took the discussion up at this point, and devoted considerable time to the environmental standards in the Terrace Galleries, particularly the change from a 35% winter minimum relative humidity to 25%. Why had this change been made? Did the new building mechanical system in fact have the capability of providing a better climate in the Terrace Galleries? It was explained that the mechanical system itself was not the problem; the constraint was wall construction. Given appropriate insulation in the outside walls of the Terrace Galleries and an air-lock between the new and old parts of the building, the expected relative humidity range of 35% to 50% could have been provided. However, given the choice between a base climate of 35% to 50%RH with a space-consuming, forbidding air-lock, and a base climate of 25% to 50%RH with micro-climates for sensitive artifacts, the ECTF had decided to opt for the latter. It was unanimously agreed by workshop participants that it was extremely important that the exterior walls of the new Terrace Galleries be constructed to handle higher relative humidity levels whether in large micro-climates adjacent to the walls or, if this were later desired, in the entire gallery. It must be noted that conservation professionals present at the workshop felt that a minimum relative humidity limit as low as 25% was not satisfactory.

b) THE ATRIUM SPACES

Reservations were expressed by the workshop participants about the architects' concept of an atrium space between the old and new construction, as it seems to pose conservation problems. The atrium spaces, which will have a total of 12,000 square feet of floor space and be four storeys high, will be used not only for visitor circulation, but are also intended as display space. However, a multi-storey glass-roofed space creates its own climate, and this may not be an ideal one. The building environmental control system is designed to provide controlled environmental conditions only at the first floor level where displays will actually take place. At all other levels the atrium spaces will essentially be closed off from the adjacent galleries. The north atrium will be serviced by the north wing's first floor environmental control units, and the south atrium by the corresponding south units.

As 25% of the roofs of the four atrium spaces will be glass, heat generated by sunlight and display lighting will accumulate at the upper levels; an exhaust fan, triggered by high temperature (31°C/88°F), will be used to dispel this heat. The fact that a temperature of 31°C may be reached before the roof exhaust fan is activated will effect the relative humidity in the upper reaches in an unpredictable manner. Fears were raised that the heat buildup and humidity could produce a "greenhouse" atmosphere with large temperature and relative humidity swings between day and night, an environment suitable only for the most insensitive artifacts. However, microclimates could be provided at ground level in the atrium spaces as elsewhere in the building.

With respect to lighting, it was evident that only artifacts insensitive to light could be displayed in the atrium spaces and the areas immediately adjoining them unless special measures were taken to protect them. Lighting levels will have to be lowered in graduated steps from the brightly lit atrium spaces to the surrounding galleries so that visitors' eyes adjust comfortably. Hence care will have to be exercised in the selection of artifacts for the galleries adjacent to the atrium spaces and in the atrium spaces and in the design of these galleries.

c) ESCALATORS

The problem of escalators in the north atrium was briefly introduced. It was felt to be essential that there be a physical screen between escalators and the spaces they serve. They raise general noise levels and can cause traffic problems through breakdown or children playing. They also are a security threat because they cannot be closed off. Isolating the escalator area with screen walls would make it easier to maintain the base climate in adjacent gallery areas by reducing solar load from the atrium skylights and the effects of uncontrolled climate in the upper atrium.

d) PLANTS

One of the features of the architects' plans for the new construction is large quantities of greenery in the atrium spaces, the Terrace Galleries, and gallery rest areas. Although plants provide visual relief, in museums they can create conservation problems. Bacteria in the soil and on the plants can attack organic artifacts. Mould cultures can spread because their spores are too small for the air system's filters. The moisture and carbon dioxide plants give off can cause atmospheric hazes which are, in fact, a form of air pollution. Water vapour is especially a problem, because it raises the relative humidity in the immediate vicinity of the plant. The excessive local moisture presents a danger to any moisture-sensitive artifacts, expecially metallic objects. In addition, particles such as spores can travel on the tiny droplets of water which are only 0.3 microns in diameter, and thus cannot be filtered out by the proposed on-floor units. In the atrium spaces these problems would be decreased if these areas had their own air-handling systems, but instead, they are to be served by the recirculating units in the north and south wings. Plants need plenty of light, and light that contains ultraviolet radiation. (Plants use light in wavelengths from 300 to 800 nanometres. For engineering purposes the ultraviolet portion of the spectrum extends from 10 to 400 nanometres.) Museum artifacts need protection from light, and especially from the ultraviolet end of the spectrum. For the latter reason, the architects have provided ultraviolet filtration on all windows and on the atrium skylights. If fluorescent "grow" lights are to be provided to keep the plants flourishing, this would re-introduce the problems of strong light and ultraviolet radiation. If incandescent bulbs are used for the same purpose, the heat load on the air-conditioning system would also be increased. The issue of plants was left with some caution as to their use, concomitant with recognition of the attractiveness of plants to the public.

e) BIRDS

The Ornithology Department's gallery proposal for a flight cage for live birds was also discussed. It was noted that birds, like plants, generate particulate and pest problems and bacteria. It was agreed that if a flight cage were to be installed, it would require a separate micro-climate, that is, totally enclosed with an independent air circulation system.

f) INSECT CONTROL

Questions were raised by workshop participants regarding the major changes in overall relative humidity levels which will take place under the new environmental controls. It was pointed out that sustained increases in humidity have been found to increase the level of pest activity. However, the systems are being designed so that every gallery zone can be separately fumigated and the fumigant exhausted through a system of pipes separate from the air-handling system. Thus, if pests became a problem, they could be dealt with.

g) LIGHTING

Other issues raised by workshop participants included ambient lighting levels in the galleries and the heating effect these can have on the environment. It was pointed out that the mechanical systems were being designed to deal with the heat from an average ambient lighting level of 5 watts per square foot and a peak gallery lighting level of 7 watts per square foot. Fifteen watts per square foot could be handled in some areas but not as an overall level. The designers present agreed that these were acceptable specifications. The engineers at the workshop confirmed that micro-climate units would be able to handle the heat generated by lighting at these levels.

h) RATE OF CHANGE OF RELATIVE HUMIDITY

The rate at which the changeover from existing conditions to new climate controls takes place was also of some concern, for rapid changes in climate are very detrimental to artifacts. It was agreed that the changeover must be accomplished a few percentage points at a time over an extended period, in order to give artifacts time to adjust. The rate of change is to be controlled by the Conservation Department. Similar procedures will be necessary in changing over from summer to winter conditions and vice versa. It was suggested at the workshop that the Conservation Department be designated as the responsible authority for controlling and administering these changeovers.

D. Sensitivities of Collections

Information on the scale and diversity of the ROM's collections was provided in the background information sent to all participants prior to the workshop. Workshop participants were also given a tour of galleries and storage areas to familiarize them directly with the collections. In order to identify conservation problems more clearly with respect to environmental conditions, preliminary categories of artifact sensitivities to light, temperature, and relative humidity were prepared by the Conservation Department for the workshop. These categories were based on the climates that will be available after expansion and renovation. According to information available during the planning of the workshop the base climate in the new Curatorial Centre and Terrace Galleries would have a relative humidity range of 35% to 50%; the base climate for the existing building would have a relative humidity range of 25% to 50%.

The ROM Conservation Department also had previously produced several documents to assist the curators in deciding how to deal with the problem of artifact sensitivities in storage, study, and display areas. These documents were excerpted and refined for the purposes of the workshop, and were tabled for discussion. As a result of the workshop discussion, the categories of artifact sensitivities were further refined and are presented below.

1. SENSITIVITY OF MATERIALS TO LIGHT

Light, and especially the invisible ultraviolet component of light, causes materials to deteriorate through complex photochemical reactions. It fades pigments and dyes; in the presence of oxygen and moisture it embrittles, weakens, and discolours textiles and cellulosic materials such as paper; it rots silk. Over long periods of time or at high

levels, it can also harm by creating excessively high temperatures or rapid temperature changes in and around artifacts, causing dangerous expansion and contraction, warping
and embrittlement, and accelerating the process of deterioration from any other cause.

a) CATEGORIES OF LIGHT SENSITIVITY

The ROM Conservation Department has divided categories of
artifacts into three groups according to their sensitivity
to damage by light and ultraviolet radiation, and has recommended maximum lighting levels, ultraviolet filtration,
and display periods as appropriate:

MATERIAL	RECOMMENDED LEVELS	DISPLAY PERIOD
Group I		
Insensitive Materials		
metal stone ceramics glass	maximum 1,000 lux (100 foot candles), with heat filters	no limit
Group II		
Moderately Sensitive Materials		
varnished oil and egg tempera paintings all organic material other than that included in Group III	maximum 150 lux (15 foot candles), ultraviolet filtration	medium term: 3 to 5 years
Group III		
Extremely Sensitive Materials		
textiles, especially silk watercolours and pastels paper illuminated manuscripts and books dyed leather feathers vegetable-dyed material paintings using mixed or contemporary techniques, or unstable materials unvarnished egg tempera paintings lacquer and lacquered objects felt pen ink	maximum 50 lux (5 foot candles) ultraviolet filtration	short term: 3 to 6 months, no more than once every 5 years

b) <u>LIGHTING STANDARDS</u>

The ROM's lighting categories were discussed. They are based on British standards, which are approved by ICOM (International Council of Museums). American standards tend to be more lenient, allowing 80 to 100 lux for textiles and 100 to 120 lux for watercolours on long-term display (220 lux for four to six weeks), but the British standard seems to be more widely accepted internationally. It was pointed out that total darkness is recommended for storage areas. One material was mentioned as being super-sensitive to light - felt pen ink, used by some contemporary artists, can fade visibly in two weeks at 100 lux.

c) <u>THE USE OF LOW LIGHT LEVELS</u>

The problems for museum visitors presented with very low light levels were discussed. It has been found that if light levels are gradually reduced as the visitor proceeds through an exhibit, his eyes will more easily adjust to the lower levels. By using this method in an exhibition of Irish art, ("Treasures of Early Irish Art", 1500 B.C. to A.D. 1500), the Metropolitan Museum of Art in New York had successfully displayed the eighth century Book of Kells at the exceptionally low light level of 25 lux. In order to make the walls of the gallery more visible in the semi-darkness they were decorated with light-coloured graphics.

Some useful suggestions for lowering light levels were put forward. Black spray paint on bulbs and on cross-hatched screening below the lights has been found to work. Low voltage lamps were strongly recommended over rheostats. If rheostats are used to turn down high voltage lamps there is a colour shift towards orange, and more infrared radiation and heat are generated.

2. <u>SENSITIVITY OF MATERIALS TO RELATIVE HUMIDITY AND TEMPERATURE LEVELS AND CHANGES</u>

a) <u>RELATIVE HUMIDITY</u>

A vital factor in the preservation of museum artifacts is

relative humidity - the ratio of the amount of water vapour present to the amount needed to saturate the same volume of air at the same temperature. Low relative humidities are damaging, especially to hygroscopic materials. These materials have a permanent affinity for moisture and are constantly seeking equilibrium with the relative humidity of their environment; when humidity levels are below 35% at room temperature, they dry out, shrink, and embrittle. Hygroscopic materials include all forms of cellulose (e.g., wood, paper, cotton, linen) and all animal tissues (e.g., leather, parchment, silk, glue, bone, ivory). These same materials are also vulnerable to high humidity conditions (over 65%). Moulds appear, adhesives weaken, wood swells and distorts, and paper becomes stained. High relative humidity also encourages corrosion in metallic objects, resulting in irreversible damage from such conditions as bronze disease, and accelerates the deterioration of unstable glass.

The most important consideration in regard to relative humidity is that sudden or extreme changes must be avoided. The attempt by moisture-sensitive materials to respond to rapid change will cause artifacts to warp and joints to loosen. Thin layers of hygroscopic materials of different densities, such as ivory, marquetry, and paint or lacquer, are often cracked or flaked off by the movement of the underlying material or of any of the layers, as each layer may have a different co-efficient of expansion.

Many materials have the elasticity to withstand seasonal changes as great as 20%. It should be realized that the reactions of artifacts to changing conditions are not consistent - moisture-sensitive artifacts can lose a significant part of their moisture content after twelve to forty-eight hours of dry conditions, but reversing the process can take months or even years in an ideal environment.

b) TEMPERATURE

Temperature is almost as important to the condition of artifacts as is relative humidity. Changes in temperature cause expansion and contraction in metals and to a lesser extent in other materials according to their ability to conduct heat. If artifacts are composed of thin layers, or if they are of metal in combination with a non-metallic material, the differing rates of expansion and contraction can cause the object to warp or break apart. Extreme heat will dry out organic materials to almost the same extent as continuous exposure to low relative humidity. Even more crucial a consideration is the rule of thumb that the rate of chemical change caused by heat is doubled for every 10°C (18°F) rise in temperature.

c) <u>CATEGORIES OF SENSITIVITY</u>

Guidelines had also been established by the ROM Conservation Department to categorize artifacts according to their requirements for temperature and relative humidity levels and stability.

<u>Group I: Able to Tolerate Variable Conditions</u>

RH   25% winter minimum
            50% summer maximum $\pm$ 10% RH daily

Temp.   21° to 23.5°C (70° to 76°F)

These conditions will be provided in the existing building and the Terrace Galleries.

- ceramics

- unpolychromed stone and marble

- gold and silver

- stable glass

<u>Group II: Require Stable Conditions</u>

RH   35% winter minimum
            50% summer maximum $\pm$ 6% RH daily

Temp.   21° to 23.5°C (70° to 76°F)

These conditions will be available in the Curatorial Centre, and can be made available in Exhibition Hall.

This category includes organic materials not found in Group III, and protected metals. Guns are included because of their wood and other organic content, and paintings on canvas because of the nature of their supports.

- wood furniture, other than that in Group III

- polychromed wood

- objects of wood, bark, tapa, straw, grass, and other cellulosic materials

- papier mâché

- paper and papyrus, including works of art on paper, documents, etc.

- rare books, leather bookbindings

- textiles and costumes, except those with metallic embroidery or attachments

- oil paintings on canvas

- armour (oiled)

- guns

- Japanese sword blades (in original sheath)

- objects and garments of leather, parchment, rawhide and skin

- bone, horn, and antler

- ivory, including miniature paintings and teeth

Group III: Require Extremely Stable Conditions ("Critical")

RH   50% $\pm$ 2% RH daily

Temp.   21° to 23.5°C (70° to 76°F)

These objects are made from thin layers and/or combined organic materials, which are highly sensitive to change, and will require micro-climates.

- inlaid, gilded, and lacquered furniture

- wooden musical instruments

- panel paintings on wood, including icons

- illuminated manuscripts (paper and parchment)

- Oriental lacquer

- Japanese screens

Group IV: Require Dry Conditions

RH   minimum 20%

                maximum 35%

Temp.   21° to 23.5°C (70° to 76°F)

- iron and steel

- archaeological bronze

- unstable lead

- unstable or iridescent glass

- textiles with metallic attachments

- mummified remains

Group V: Require Cool Conditions

RH   30% $\pm$ 5% RH

Temp.   4°C $\pm$ 1° (40°F $\pm$ 2°)

- fur and fur-trimmed garments

- birdskin garments

- animal skins

- mounted bird and mammal specimens

Discussion was invited on the above categories. The problem of artifacts made of mixed materials was introduced, for example an oil painting (Group II) with a gilded frame (Group I). It was decided that the primary component (the painting) would have to be considered first. Where there is no primary component, either a compromise has to be reached or one of the materials has to be protected. The latter is possible with guns; the metal may be protected from the higher humidities required for the wood.

Concern was expressed about the 6% daily variation in relative humidity allowed in Group II, for a change that large in the space of a day can cause irreparable cracking, warping or flaking in organic materials. It was pointed out by the participating engineers that the 6% tolerance referred to the air quality only; because the objects through their bulk offer resistance to moisture movement (hysterisis), their own resulting moisture loss or gain will occur much more slowly and thus more safely. However, the conservators made the point that it is the <u>attempt</u> of objects to change that causes the damage. This includes temperature change, which can cause metals to expand or contract and damage organic material combined with them.

3. <u>THE NEED FOR MICRO-CLIMATES</u>

Workshop participants were provided with a summary sheet of the proportions of collections in each of the categories of artifact sensitivities (Matrix #1). In this chart, departments are grouped into conceptually related "clusters", as described in the final ECTF report, <u>Mankind Discovering</u>. Gallery planning up to the time of the workshop was based on this cluster concept. The chart had two objectives:

(1)   to identify the percentages of departmental collections with the greatest sensitivities to relative humidity, temperature, and light, and,

(2)   to explore the possibility of locating collections according to conditions provided by the expected base climates.

It should be noted that the percentages in the chart represent percentages of each collection; they are not percentages of the total ROM collection. For example, 10% of the Far Eastern collection would require much more space than 10% of the comparatively small European Archaeology collection.

This analysis had revealed that in fact the number of the ROM's artifacts requiring special conditions was not nearly as great as had originally been thought. The problem had thus become more manageable. A rough calculation indicated that sensitive artifacts represented approximately 10% to 15% of the total collections. Thus a small but significant proportion of the ROM's collections requires enhanced environments, that is, beyond that provided by the new base climate. These artifacts will require special micro-climates.

Matrix #1: Analysis of Department Collections

DEPARTMENT	PERCENTAGE OF COLLECTIONS SENSITIVE TO RH AND TEMPERATURE BY CLIMATE TYPE					PERCENTAGE SENSITIVE TO LIGHT BY MAXIMUM LUX LEVELS		
	I variable	II stable	III critical	IV dry	V cool	I 300	II 150	III 50
Mediterranean Basin								
European Archaeology	80	–	–	20	–	100	–	–
Greek and Roman	85	–	–	15	–	100	–	–
Egyptian	48	50	–	2	–	50	50	–
West Asian	83	13	2	2	–	85	8	7
Europe/Canada								
European	20	58	22	–	–	20	70	10
Textiles	15	78	–	–	7	–	7	93
Canadiana	40	50	10	–	–	25	40	35
New World								
North American Archaeology	100	–	–	–	–	100	–	–
Central American Archaeology	99	–	1	–	–	100	–	–
South American Archaeology	100	–	–	–	–	100	–	–
Ethnology	15	77	3	–	5	15	60	25
Far Eastern	72	15	3	10	–	70	25	5

DEPARTMENT	PERCENTAGE OF COLLECTIONS SENSITIVE TO RH AND TEMPERATURE BY CLIMATE TYPE					PERCENTAGE SENSITIVE TO LIGHT BY MAXIMUM LUX LEVELS		
	I variable	II stable	III critical	IV dry	V cool	I 300	II 150	III 50
Life Sciences								
Botany	100	–	–	–		100	–	–
Entomology	100	–	–	–	–	–	75	25
Invertebrate Zoology	100	–	–	–	–	50	50	–
Ichthyology	100	–	–	–	–	–	100	–
Herpetology	100	–	–	–	–	–	98	2
Ornithology	97	1	–	–	2	–	80	20
Mammalogy	97	–	–	–	3	–	100	–
Palaeontology								
Vertebrate	100	–	–	–	–	–	100	–
Invertebrate	100	–	–	–	–	95	–	5
Earth Sciences								
Mineralogy	98	–	–	2	–	95	–	5
Geology	100	–	–	–	–	100	–	–
Planetarium	100	–	–	–	–	100	–	–

A second chart of 10 pages, "Mixing of Artifacts of Varying Sensitivities" (Matrix #2; see sample pages below), was also presented to workshop participants. This chart identified, by proposed gallery, where there would likely be mixing of artifacts with different environmental requirements. The solid dots in circles (●) indicate especially difficult mixing problems.

Matrix #2 Mixing of Artifacts of Varying Sensitivities (sample)

PROPOSED GALLERIES	LIKELY COMBINATIONS OF ARTIFICTS OF VARYING RH SENSITIVITIES							LIKELY COMBINATIONS OF ARTIFACTS OF VARYING LIGHT SENSITIVITIES				
	LIKELY SENSITIVITIES (BY GROUP)					PROBABILITY OF MIX		LIKELY SENSITIVITIES (BY GROUP)			PROBABILITY OF MIX	
	I Variable	II Stable	III Critical	IV Dry	V Cool	High	Low	I 300	II 150	III 50	High	Low
Far Eastern (cont'd)												
Mediaeval China	• tomb figures			• mirrors		•		•	• painted figures		•	
High-fired Mono-chrome	• ceramics						•	•				•
Stoneware: Sung-Ming	• ceramics						•	•	•			•
Ming & China Porcelain	• ceramics						•	•				•
Chinese Furniture		• furniture, textiles	• lacquer			•				• textiles, paintings	•	
Ming & Ching Decorative Arts	• ceramics	• red lacquer	• Inlaid lacquer, musical Instruments			•		•	•		•	
Chinese & Japanese Pictorial Arts		• paintings					•			•		•

Matrix #2 (continued)

PROPOSED GALLERIES	LIKELY COMBINATIONS OF ARTIFACTS OF VARYING RH SENSITIVITIES							LIKELY COMBINATIONS OF ARTIFACTS OF VARYING LIGHT SENSITIVITIES				
	LIKELY SENSITIVITIES (BY GROUP)					PROBABILITY OF MIX		LIKELY SENSITIVITIES (BY GROUP)			PROBABILITY OF MIX	
	I Variable	II Stable	III Critical	IV Dry	V Cool	High	Low	I 300	II 150	III 50	High	Low
Japanese Dec. Art & Ceramics	● ceramics	● textiles, wooden sculpture	● screens, lacquer	● swords		◉		●		●	●	
● Asian Buddhist Arts	● stone	● wood carvings, paintings, silk, paper	● polychrome wood	● Iron, bronze		◉		●	●	●	●	
● India	● stone	● wood		● bronze		◉		●		●	●	

Matrix #2 showed that the Science collections rarely mixed artifacts of varying sensitivities; it was the Art and Archaeology galleries that would be most problematic, especially artifacts from historic periods (non-archaeological). For example, pieces from the Textile Department will be found in most of the Art and Archaeology galleries, and they are in Group II (requiring stable conditions). It was agreed that if textiles form a minor portion of a gallery containing mostly Group I type objects (able to withstand variable conditions) they be enclosed in microclimates.

Matrix #2 also showed that the heaviest concentration of Group I (insensitive) material outside of the science departments is the ceramics and silver in the European Department.

It was noted that according to Matrix #1 the major portion of artifacts needing higher relative humidities was found in the European collections. It was also noted that these artifacts are often displayed in period room settings and are likely best dealt with as total areas screened from the public ("micro-rooms"). It was pointed out that if these rooms were independent of outside walls of the building, their location would not have to be in the Terrace Galleries.

Group IV (dry climate) artifacts tend to be bronzes, which in the Far Eastern Department occupy entire galleries. A mechanical dry air system, split among bronze galleries, was suggested, but discarded because in the summer this would have to be a major system with special cooling coils for dehumidifying outside air. Another suggestion was that a dry air supply be taken from the dry storage area in the Curatorial Centre, but this was considered impractical because of the distances involved.

The idea was explored that galleries be organized according to the senistivity of the materials, and many alternatives were brought forward. The ideal of one prime climate area which would house all the sensitive (Group III) material was mentioned, but discarded, as the artifacts in this category involve large areas of the European and Far Eastern galleries, and are also scattered into many smaller groups within other departments.

A radical proposal was made that the idea of overall base climates be given up and all artifacts be kept in microclimates, leaving the public environment to make do with leakage from the cases. It would be an expensive system to build, but would require a smaller volume of controlled air, thus saving money in the long run. This, however, would provide an unacceptable climate for Museum visitors. The engineers also pointed out that the <u>cost and energy effective use of micro-climates is predicated upon the availability of a reasonable base climate</u>.

An approach to the use of micro-climates was beginning to emerge, and can be summarized as follows:

- Given an out-of-date building, an extreme outdoor climate, and a relatively small proportion of artifacts requiring special conditions, it is more cost- and energy-efficient to provide micro-climates for the artifacts themselves rather than for the building, as a whole or in part.

- Climates suitable for artifacts are not necessarily comfortable for the visitor.

- New museum construction (walls, roofs, etc.) should be built to handle the best possible internal environmental conditions, even if those conditions are not to be made available immediately.

- Heating effects from gallery lighting and solar load through windows and skylights must be taken into consideration during design of mechanical systems.

- Plants and animals are not recommended for use or display in museums, unless enclosed in independent micro-climates.

- Fumigation of galleries should be allowed for by including a separate exhaust system in the mechanical plans.

- Escalators should be screened off from gallery areas.

- Areas of low light level should be approached by museum visitors through progressively darker galleries.

- Low voltage lamps are preferred to high voltage lamps on rheostats (dimmers) for creating low light levels.

- Mixed-material artifacts should be placed in micro-climates suited to the primary component or components which cannot be protected from adverse relative humidity.

- Daily variations in relative humidity should be kept as small as possible.

● Planned changes in relative humidity must be carried out in gradual steps over an extended period of time, preferably under the supervision of a conservator.

● Large groups of artifacts requiring similar micro-climates should be gathered together where possible in "micro-rooms", large micro-climate areas screened off from the public.

E. The Use of Micro-Climates

1. EXISTING SOLUTIONS

The workshop participants were supplied with an annotated bibliography selected to illustrate the state of the art of micro-climates up to the present. This bibliography is presented at the end of this report. The environmental control methods discussed in the references were summarized as follows:

Relative Humidity and Temperature

Physical barriers or enclosures

- building within a building

- types of wall construction materials and coverings (e.g., adiabatic, impermeable)

- sealed cases with or without various gases

- ventilation holes and filters

- ratio between object size and case volume

- "breathing" cases

Buffers

- sorbent materials in case construction (e.g., wood, particle board, cloth lining)

48

- saturated salt solutions:

  - lithium chloride

  - sodium bromide

  - magnesium nitrate hexahydrate

- inorganic hygroscopic materials:

  - zeolite

  - silica gel

  - kaken gel (Nikka pellets)

- organic hygroscopic materials:

  - wood shavings

  - woods of low specific gravity

- container paint colour as a heat buffer

Mechanical Methods

- evaporation-type humidifier

- heat pump type of dehumidifier

- thermo-electric and vapour cycle

- modification to air-conditioning and atomizers

Dust and Pollutants Control

- air cleaners (4 types)

- zeolite

- curing time of new concrete

- traffic control

Light and Heat, and General Environment bibliographies were not summarized.

a) BUFFERS

The use of buffers to assist in producing micro-climates was discussed. Workshop participants first attempted to sort out which existing solutions might be applicable. The most common current method for creating micro-climates is through the use of absorbents such as silica gel. Silica gel can be used as either a buffer, a desiccant, or a humidifier. The gel, which is basically expanded silicon dioxide, readily takes on moisture. Used as a desiccant in a closed space, it will absorb up to 300 grams of moisture per kilogram of gel, thus maintaining a dry environment. Used in such a manner, it must be removed periodically and dried for twelve hours in an oven, as it can only adsorb so much moisture before it becomes saturated. As a humidifier, it can be pretreated by exposing it to a damp environment for three to seven days and then placed in a dry closed space. It will give off its adsorbed moisture until it becomes dried out, requiring retreatment. It can act as a self-conditioning buffer because it adsorbs or releases moisture during rapid changes in relative humidity. more readily than the object it is protecting, thus moderating and slowing down extreme changes. For example, if the outside relative humidity drops to 25%, the case may only reach a low of 30% before the relative humidity starts to rise again.

Because of the cost, time, and manpower involved in maintenance, silica gel was found to be impractical for unsealed or large cases. Over a period of time the relative humidity in an unsealed case will come to match the mean relative humidity of the surrounding gallery. There is also a limit on the size of micro-climate that can be conditioned by silica gel. A micro-climate using a static system would need unmanageably large quantities of silica gel; one using a dynamic (fan) system would require the silica gel to be spread over a very wide area.

The materials used in constructing cases can in themselves act as buffers. Organic hygroscopic (moisture-absorbing) materials, such as wood and Tentest, can be used for this purpose. Old-fashioned walnut cases used in the ROM are remarkably effective in slowing moderate fluctuations of relative humidity. Such materials can be used in case construction, flooring, or panelling within a case. Paint acts as a barrier to moisture, but caution must be used as some acrylics contain corrosive sulphur.

It was emphasized in discussion that materials used in cases must be pretested for their effect on artifacts; certain dye colours, for example, have been found to contain sulphur only after they have tarnished all the silver in a case.

A large hygroscopic object in a small case is not an appropriate subject for a buffer, as the object itself affects so strongly the air around it. It was pointed out that moving things into a case during the winter could be a problem. The relative humidity to which the artifact had adjusted in controlled storage conditions might be widely different from that of the air in the case. It was suggested that some Group III materials be moved only once or twice a year, preferably at times of optimum relative humidity.

Questions were raised about the quantities of buffer needed; these would be dependent on case leak rate, buffering qualities of display materials, temperature control, and whether a static or dynamic system were used. A portable micro-climate module was suggested to maintain case conditions while it was open for changing displays. It was noted that while the climate of a small case would be seriously disturbed by opening it, it could be reconditioned that much more quickly. There was unanimous agreement that case access be strictly limited.

Buffers would be impractical for cases containing a large volume of air in relation to the volume of the artifacts. Large quantities of buffer material would be needed, thus requiring a case strong enough to bear the load. (A ratio of 20 kg per cubic metre/1.25 lb. per cubic foot in a non-permeable case has been established.)

Workshop participants thought that buffers would be unsuitable for cases which have a volume greater than 1,000 cubic feet because of the sheer difficulty of maintenance, especially if they are not airtight. The quantity of silica gel could be reduced if it was spread over removable panels to increase the surface area, and if a fan system was added. Cases would have to be designed to allow the panels to be removed regularly for re-conditioning without seriously altering the internal climate.

Participants were asked whether there are circumstances where buffers are preferable to mechanical systems. It was admitted that they needed practically no maintenance in a static system, because the material can withstand minor fluctuations, and they are ideal in terms of energy saving. Buffers could perhaps be used as a portable alternate system

to complement mechanically conditioned cases. They have the
added advantage of being able to cope with sudden relative
humidity changes caused by temperature fluctuations.

It was generally agreed that buffers can be useful but
should not be relied upon extensively. Their use should be
determined according to individual micro-climate requirements. Buffers could be most effective for short-term exhibits. In such circumstances the extra labour required
would be minimal.

b) MECHANICAL SOLUTIONS

A discussion was held on the availability of existing mechanical solutions. The suggestion was made that some of the
environmental requirements might be handled as extensions
of the proposed five-zone mechanical system for the whole
Museum. It was noted that using ducting from the mechanical
system would severely limit flexibility in changing displays.
However, for more permanent displays, like period rooms,
this appeared a reasonable approach, if it were possible.

Mr. Arthur Jones, the consulting mechanical engineer, calculated that extra humidification of large areas such as period rooms could be handled by a separate recirculatory cooling and humidification system. The conditioned areas would
be sealed and separated from the outside walls. Energy savings would be made by recycling the humidified air. The
cost was calculated at roughly $1,500 per humidification
unit, but labour costs for the ductwork could be twice as
much.

The need for display flexibility, the size of the ducts, and
the cost of providing ducting and a larger supply of outside
air made this solution appropriate only for larger areas.
It was suggested that several period rooms be grouped together in one wing for greater efficiency. However, only four
separate areas in the Museum were defined as needing such a
system.

Drying mechanisms could be built into the system, but they
were seen to be expensive. As mostly smaller objects needed
to be kept dry, individual case units seemed more practical.

2. NEW SOLUTIONS

The existing solutions (buffers, mechanical, etc.) had been considered in the context of the ROM's environmental conditions, its collections, and its display requirements. The discussion centred on whether any of the existing solutions would be appropriate, and from there moved on to the consideration of possible new solutions. The two main subjects were:

- definition and establishment of requirements for case designs for varying conditions and specifications

- requirements and specifications for mechanical solutions. This topic covered actual "black box" parameters such as:

  - capacity

  - supply requirements (water and power)

  - physical housing limitations

  - noise

  - maintenance

  - aesthetic design requirements

  - size

a) DISPLAY CASES

In preparation for the workshop the Exhibit Design Services Department at the ROM had prepared a list of display unit module sizes.

- small   —   10 cubic feet
                  50 cubic feet
                  100 cubic feet

- medium   – 200 cubic feet

                      400 cubic feet

                      1,000 cubic feet

- diorama, small period room – 3,000 cubic feet

- period room   – 7,000 cubic feet

                      14,000 cubic feet

- gallery   –20,000 cubic feet

Participants discussed whether the case unit sizes identified are reasonable modules to work with in creating micro-
climates. Three ranges of case size satisfactory to the
Exhibit Design Services Department and appropriate for equipment design were agreed upon: 10 to 50 cubic feet, 100 to
200 cubic feet, and 400 to 1,000 cubic feet. Equipment could
be designed so that several pieces of equipment can be used
in parallel to deal with larger volumes if necessary. With
this range of cases and accompanying equipment, it should
be possible to deal with most instances where there will be
artifacts of differing sensitivities in one gallery.

The Exhibit Design Services Department also listed for the
participants questions regarding the construction of display
units.

- Should display units be completely sealed and, if so,
  with what type of seal?

- What is the effect of different case materials on the
  micro-climates to be provided?

- How does the requirement for accessibility to display
  units affect the maintaining of micro-climates, taking
  into consideration:

  (a) frequency of access

  (b) size of opening

  (c) ease of access

This accessibility should be considered for the following
conditions:

  (a) removal of material for short-term study or treatment
      purposes

(b) short-term displays, three to six months

(c) medium-term displays, three to five years

(d) permanent displays

● What guidelines should be established for the location, density, and type of light fixtures?

What Materials are Appropriate for Sealed Cases?

During the brief discussion of suitable materials for a sealed case, standard window technology was cited as a criterion. Wood was considered acceptable if it were sealed (e.g., with varnish or paint) to offset its permeability.

Some participants expressed concern about effective sealing at access doors. Others felt that the main problem was the glass/frame joints, but it was agreed that a suitable joint could be accomplished. The use of Plexiglas and other acrylic plastics was discussed. There was no concern about their permeability to moisture, but they are too scratch-prone for use within touching distance of the public. There are scratch-resistant plastics, but they are not as clear as the standard type.

It was generally felt that the technology for building airtight cases is available and the next step should be to build and test such cases to determine what is possible in terms of leak-rate. When this has been determined, micro-climate equipment (black boxes) can be designed accordingly. It was decided that the engineers and designers would have to work together in the development of the equipment and the design of the cases so that the two would interface effectively.

The Use of Sealed Cases

A major issue that emerged with respect to new mechanical equipment for creating micro-climates was the cost of designing airtight (low-leakage) cases. It was pointed out by the participating engineers that the lower the leak rate, the more cost effective and mechanically simple the equipment could be, because less make-up air would have to be introduced. This was so, whether the equipment was to humidify, desiccate, or cool. It was agreed that in general the equipment needed to provide drier climates and cooler temperatures is relatively easy to provide. On the other hand, more complicated and expensive equipment is needed for maintaining higher humidity levels.

In contrast to airtight cases, the leaking system used in the Egyptian Galleries at the Metropolitan Museum of Art in New York was described. This is a system in which appropriately conditioned air is introduced first into a micro-climate and then is leaked into the base environment. It was felt that if self-contained mechanical equipment were used, this system would be too energy-expensive to provide large micro-climates.

It was noted by both the conservators and the designers that few attempts have been made to create airtight cases. Traditionally the concern has been to create dust-free cases in which air transfer was desirable. Without a black box to adjust the climate within a case, it has been preferable to develop leaking cases. The use of a sealed case would also be questionable if there were no way of accommodating factors such as heat buildup from outside sources.

Accessibility

There would be little point in creating a special non-leaking micro-climate if the case were constantly being opened. It was decided that access must be limited and that the only way to ensure this would be for it to be controlled by the Conservation Department. It was agreed that where access is required at regular intervals, mechanical solutions are more appropriate than solutions using buffers. Buffers would take much longer to re-establish required conditions.

b) LIGHTING

All aspects of lighting were discussed, covering types of lamps and fixtures, their placement in relation to the case, heat buildup, and the effect of lights on the stability of internal case climates. The ROM categories of materials graded according to light sensitivity, and the lighting standards were reviewed and confirmed by the workshop participants.

Heat Buildup

As far as micro-climates were concerned, it was agreed in

discussion that wherever possible all lights should be outside display cases in order to prevent the buildup of internal heat generated by light fixtures. It was also noted
that where lighting is unavoidable within micro-climates,
low voltage fixtures on low voltage equipment should be used
to reduce heat. Fixtures such as rheostats which reduce
voltage are not as effective, as they tend to heat up. It
was acknowledged that any mechanical equipment for micro-
climates would have to be designed to cope with the effects
of spot-light, infrared radiation being absorbed by dark-
coloured artifacts, and heating them up while leaving the
case air temperature relatively unchanged.

Ways of reducing heat buildup from lighting were suggested.
Good quality anti-heat lenses could be used to stop infrared radiation without affecting the light quality; the light
could also be bounced off the back of its holder. Local
transformers could be used on top of cases for low-voltage
fixtures. The cases themselves could contain screened vents
to allow heat to escape, and possibly also whisper fans, although they are subject to breakdown.

The consulting mechanical engineer would like the lights to
be built into the false ceiling; in this way the air flow
of the building mechanical system can dissipate 40% of the
heat that goes upward into the plenum, saving fan energy by
recycling heated air. At the time of the workshop, gallery
lighting, which was the responsibility of the ECTF, had not
been decided, so it was impossible to say whether or not
there would be any general ceiling lighting, or indeed,
whether or not there would be a ceiling.

Temperature and Relative Humidity Variations Caused by
Diurnal Lighting Cycles

Temperature is a difficult factor to deal with, because it
has a decided effect on relative humidity levels. A rule of
thumb states that at 21°C (70°F) and 50% relative humidity,
for example, every 1.8°C (1°F) rise in temperature decreases
the relative humidity level by 1% to 1½%RH. As lights are
turned on and off in galleries, temperature fluctuates, making it difficult to maintain a constant relative humidity
inside a case.

The engineers noted that it would be easier and more cost-
effective to control humidity if the internal case temperature could be higher than the annual daytime base climate

maximum for the galleries. Lights raise the case temperature during the day and when they are turned off, the temperature drops. To maintain a diurnally constant relative humidity in a sealed case, the temperature must also be kept constant. As it is cheaper to heat than to cool, money and energy would be saved if a constant temperature could be maintained at the highest daytime level, and the cases heated at night to conform with this. Additionally, the mechanical engineers pointed out that if year-round heating of the cases was seen as a solution the use of the galleries as a heat sink might be an advantage in winter, but would raise cooling costs in summer.

However, the conservators objected vigorously to the proposal of high case temperatures, reminding the engineers of the deteriorative effects of heat on artifacts. It was then suggested that the ambient gallery temperature be lowered to 20°C (68°F), which was the coolest temperature the air-conditioning system could achieve during the summer, and the case temperature be allowed to rise to and be maintained at 25.5°C (78°F); however, conservators stated this was still unacceptably high for the artifacts.

Fluorescent Lighting

Some conservators felt that fluorescent tubes should be banned completely for light-sensitive material. Ultraviolet filtration would be needed on them in any case, as they contain 3% to 7% ultraviolet radiation as compared with incandescent lights at 1% and daylight at up to 25%. The designers present preferred low-voltage incandescent lamps for museum use, as they felt that fluorescents give a bland, diffused light unsuitable for the dramatic presentation of artifacts.

c) MONITORING

The issue of monitoring micro-climates was also discussed. Arthur Jones indicated that central computer-based electronic controls for monitoring temperature and humidity, if desired, could be incorporated into the building system now, along with the security monitoring controls. Many cautions were raised by workshop participants regarding such a system:

  - Security needs and conservation needs differ
    widely and may not be compatible.

- Sophisticated systems often fail due to lack
  of skilled maintenance. Human back-up is essential,
  and this means two overlapping well-trained
  staff members. Maintenance quality has been
  found generally to deteriorate each step it gets
  removed from the original installer. A weekly
  job sheet was suggested so that routine prevent-
  ive maintenance would be consistently carried
  out.

- There is a need for change and flexibility with
  respect to the location of many artifacts.
  Permanent displays could easily be wired into
  the monitoring system, but the majority of displays
  need to be flexible in terms of case layout.
  Some type of wireless transmitter device would
  be needed for these movable cases. This implies
  an even more complicated and expensive system.

Although the idea of central electronic controls was not totally dismissed, the general feeling of workshop participants
was that such a system has many inherent problems and other
less complicated means of monitoring should also be explored.
It was pointed out that it would be necessary to have a visual indication, such as a red light, at the problem point
when a micro-climate begins to fail, and a means of assessing
immediately the extent to which the climate has degraded.
The engineers assured the other workshop participants that
simple monitors could be built into the equipment to perform
these functions, and that indicators could also be included
to show whether the monitoring system itself was functioning.
An electronic probe-type sensor could also be built into each
case, to which a conservator could attach a read-out device
if the warning light was activated.

d) BUILDING SYSTEM FAILURE

Concern was expressed about contingency measures - what
would happen if there were a major breakdown or power failure and the systems failed? Arthur Jones assured the participants that back-up parts and duplicate pumps to two-thirds
capacity were being provided. If one of two cooling units
broke down on a peak day, the lights and outside air input
would be turned off until the remaining unit could handle
the load. Only the heating system will have an emergency
back-up, because everything else but the heating and the

chillers can be fixed before the environment degrades seriously. So far the longest power failure the ROM has experienced has lasted one hour. As there is little glass in the building and it will be well insulated, temperature loss should be no more than 1°C (1.8°F) per hour, and thus should not drastically affect the micro-climates.

Simple first aid procedures for power failures were discussed, such as enclosing micro-climates in plastic sheeting or polyurethane slabs. A silica gel back-up system was also suggested. Written down emergency procedures were strongly recommended to help preserve micro-climates as long as possible if the ambient climate failed.

e) <u>APPLICATION OF SOLUTIONS</u>

Existing and new solutions were considered in terms of the five categories of sensitivities already established. In order to define more clearly in what instances black boxes would be required, a third matrix was developed:

Matrix #3   Application of New Solutions in the ROM

Sensitivities of Materials:	Group I	Group II	Group III	Group IV	Group V
	variable	stable	"critical"	dry	cool
Artifacts in galleries (no cases)		upgraded	upgraded		
Artifacts in rooms or large cases		Building Mechanical System	Building Mechanical System	Black Box	Black Box
Artifacts in medium sized cases		Black Box	Black Box	Black Box	Black Box
Artifacts in small sized cases		Black Box	Black Box	Black Box	Black Box

3. CRITERIA FOR MICRO-CLIMATES

It became clear to workshop participants that:

1. New solutions not yet available in the marketplace were required for three different types of stable climate - moist (more humid than base relative humidity)

    - dry (less humid than base relative humidity)

    - cool (cooler than base temperature);

2. The building mechanical system could be used for humidification of larger areas such as period rooms (i.e., over 1,000 cubic feet);

3. Humidification of smaller micro-climates and all drying and cooling would have to be accomplished independently of the building mechanical system.

The remainder of the workshop discussion focused on delineating more specifically the conditions for which new mechanical solutions (black boxes) should be designed. It had been made clear by the engineers present that hardware could be designed, but it was important to ensure that it would be practical - that it not place undue constraints on display techniques, not be too costly, perform quietly, and be manageable from the point of view of maintenance and monitoring.

The possibility of a cool temperature micro-climate was suggested for fur garments and animal mounts. The engineers thought that the best that could be achieved without sweating or fogging on the exterior of the case, and without insulating or using thermal glass, would be an internal temperature of 13°C (56°F), which would still be on the point of sweating at exterior conditions of 23.5°C (76°F), 50% relative humidity. Bearing in mind this base line gallery climate, they agreed that the lowest non-fog temperature possible would be about 15.5°C (60°F). If a temperature lower than this was required the cooled case would have to be insulated with thermal glass. This would allow the temperature to be reduced to 3.5°C (40°F) or even lower. Ideally cooled fur garments require 30% relative humidity ± 5%. In order to achieve this relative humidity at lowered temperatures, some dehumidification system would have to be incorporated.

While the actual design of mechanical micro-climate systems would come later, some possible solutions were suggested at the workshop. For the dry system, a regenerative pressur- izer dehydrator in a closed case was considered (see figure 4). This would have dual chambers for a desiccant, of which one at a time would dry the case and bleed some dry air to regenerate the other; a heater device might have to be in- cluded (see figure 5). In a non-airtight case, a fan or pres- surizing device could be included to provide a slight posi- tive pressure to keep the outside relative humidity from affecting the case environment. This would be a relatively efficient dynamic system which would not need large quanti- ties of desiccant. Heat buildup from the dehydrator and the ambient lighting could be dealt with up to a maximum energy level of seven watts per square foot.

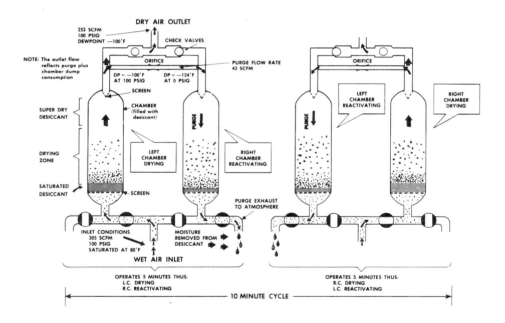

Figure 4:   Regenerative pressurizer dehydrator (reproduced with permission of the Pall Trinity Micro Corporation).

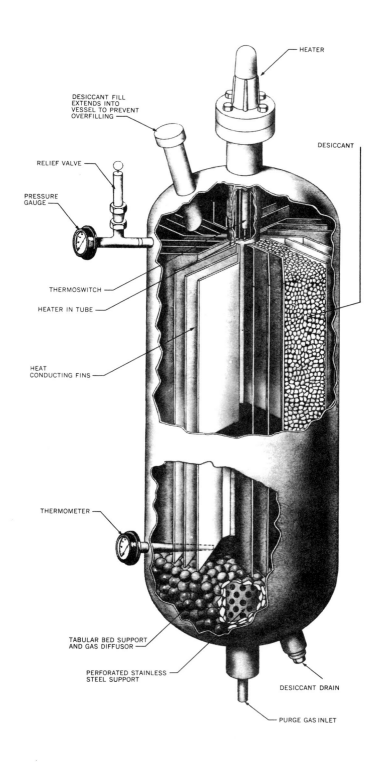

HEATER

DESICCANT FILL
EXTENDS INTO
VESSEL TO PREVENT
OVERFILLING

DESICCANT

RELIEF VALVE

PRESSURE
GAUGE

THERMOSWITCH

HEATER IN TUBE

HEAT
CONDUCTING FINS

THERMOMETER

TABULAR BED SUPPORT
AND GAS DIFFUSOR

PERFORATED STAINLESS
STEEL SUPPORT

DESICCANT DRAIN

PURGE GAS INLET

Figure 5: Typical electrically heated desiccant chamber (reproduced with permission of the Pall Trinity Micro Corporation).

With regards to a moist system, there was some discussion about water supply. Piped in water, although available in all areas of the Museum - and cheaper than the equipment for a closed system, demands an inflexible arrangement of cases and presents the danger of flooding if an overflow occurs. Automatic filling devices, however sophisticated, can fail, and a drainage system is required. A well-sealed case with a water storage tank was preferred, to be topped up manually. A small case with a one cubic foot per minute leak-rate would lose about one gallon a month, and so would need weekly topping up. A fungicide would have to be added to the water to prevent the growth of moulds.

Another problem with any humidification unit is the buildup of mineral salts and other detritus. Electrode (steam) humidifiers need undistilled water for current conductivity, and the electrodes must be replaced every 15 months or so. It was suggested that an evaporator-type humidifier (either mechanical or passive) would be preferable. It can use distilled water which lessens lime buildup and requires less maintenance; if the case is well sealed, filling can be kept to a minimum.

Part III
Recommendations and Conclusions

Part III
Recommendations and
Conclusions

The final activity of the workshop was the delineation of a
set of recommendations and conclusions. The major recommen-
dation was the need to develop new equipment - the black
boxes - which will make micro-climates feasible wherever
they are required. The parameters for such micro-climate
units were established and their specification worked out
by the engineers of Convectron Inc. and appear in Appendix
B of this report.

It is hoped that the eventual main product of this workshop
will be the broad availability of black boxes, making micro-
climates economically feasible for any institution that
needs them. The ROM hopes to develop equipment based upon
the information presented and agreed upon at the workshop.
This equipment, in conjunction with concomitant experience
in developing cases and in assembling and operating micro-
climates, should prove to be a benefit to all museums with
artifacts requiring exacting environmental conditions.

All the participants in the workshop felt strongly that
there was a need to publish both the proceedings and the
results of the workshop. It was felt that other museums
could benefit and learn from the approach being planned by
the ROM for solving its environmental problems.

The following summary of conclusions reflects the basic orientation of the workshop, which was to define approaches and
delineate practical solutions.

Recommendations

- A reasonable base climate must be provided in all galleries. (In the ROM a base climate of 25% winter minimum to 50% summer maximum relative humidity will accommodate the environmental needs of 90% of the collections.)

- The exterior walls of the new Terrace Galleries should be constructed to handle a higher relative humidity, whether in large micro-climates adjacent to the walls, or, if this were later desired, in the entire gallery.

- Micro-climates will be required to provide special environments for sensitive collections.

- Artifact need, not visitor comfort, is to determine the design of micro-climates.

- Energy conservation is of high importance, a constraint which will have to be considered at all times.

- Airtight sealed micro-climates are essential to ensure environmental stability with minimum energy waste.

Conclusions

- Extensions of the building mechanical system can be used to provide humid micro-climates for all large areas.

- Self-contained black boxes must be used for all dry, cool, and humid micro-climates under 1,000 cubic feet.

- Buffer materials are appropriate for micro-climates which are small, do not require frequent access, or are used for short-term exhibits.

- Where frequent access is required, micro-climates must have mechanical systems to maintain their environment.

- Cool ambient gallery temperatures facilitate the maintenance of stable micro-climates, while increasing energy efficiency.

Lighting

- Incandescent lights or fluorescent ballasts must be outside cases whenever possible to avoid excessive heat load within the micro-climates.

- Low-voltage lamps and low-voltage equipment are to be used for all museum displays where sensitive artifacts are shown, in order to maintain low light and heat levels without colour distortion.

Maintenance and Monitoring

- Maintenance capabilities must be provided or developed within the institution to ensure the proper operation of the mechanical equipment required to produce micro-climates.

- Monitoring systems are essential to ensure that both building climate and individual micro-climates are functioning properly.

- Contingency plans and back-up procedures to deal with mechanical breakdown of building climate and individual micro-climates must be established and tested.

- Access to cases must be restricted in order to maintain effective micro-climates. Access should be under the direct control of the Conservation Department.

- Testing under supervision of the Conservation Department is required for all micro-climate equipment before being used for sensitive artifacts.

- Distilled water storage tanks are preferable to a piped-in water supply for all cases requiring water to maintain humid micro-climates. This provides for greater flexibility in locating micro-climates and at the same time lessens the danger of flooding.

Appendices

A. The Building Mechanical System
Arthur Jones, P. Eng.

Heating for the new ROM will be provided by reclaimed building heat, supplemented by steam from the University of
Toronto. Heating will be on the outside walls, using low
temperature (40.5°C/105°F maximum) hot water through finned
tube radiation, cabinet heaters, and unit heaters. Because
artifacts cannot be wall-mounted above baseboard units, a
wall 12.7 cm (15 in.) from the exterior wall will be constructed with a 71 cm (28 in.) access panel and ventilation
spaces at top and bottom. Cooling for the Museum
will be provided by heat reclaim chillers located in the
third basement of the Curatorial Centre. Condenser heat
will be used for building heating or domestic potable hot
water heating, or will be rejected through towers on the
fifth floor roof as appropriate.

Outside ventilation air to conditioned spaces will be supplied by roof-mounted units providing fixed minimum outside air requirements year round. One ventilation air unit
will be provided to each air handling floor zone. Each air
unit will incorporate gaseous and particulate filtration,
combination heating/cooling coils, spray-type grid humidifier, and centrifugal supply air fan. Make-up air for the
64 exhausts in laboratories, workshops, and kitchen, to a
maximum of 80% of the exhaust requirement, will be provided
by non-conditioned filtered outside air, supplied from two
fan units located in the roof penthouse through ductwork to
the immediate exhaust location. This variable volume make-
up air system will include a heating coil plus high efficiency filters, and humidification can be provided for Conservation Department exhaust hoods in which humidity-sensi-
tive artifacts are treated.

According to physical layout and construction phasing, the
building will be divided into seven zones for air handling.

Each zone will have a separate mechanical system which will handle air filtration, heating or cooling, and humidification or dehumidification. Air-conditioning throughout the Museum will be provided by floor-mounted compartment units, each serving a specified zone as follows:

- North Wing, East Block   1 unit/floor

- North Wing, West Block   1 unit/floor

- Centre Block   1 unit/floor

- Terrace Galleries   1 unit/floor, all floors ex-
                               cept 4th floor, which will
                               be served from 3rd floor

- South Wing, East Block   1 unit/floor

- South Wing, West Block   1 unit/floor

- Curatorial Centre   2 units/floor

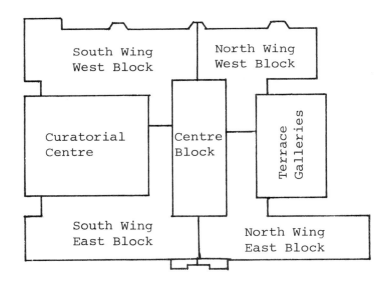

Figure 6:   Air handling zones.

The combination of outside ventilation air unit and floor-mounted compartment units is shown on figure 7.

The ventilation unit, located at roof level in a mechanical penthouse, filters, preheats, and partially humidifies, or pre-

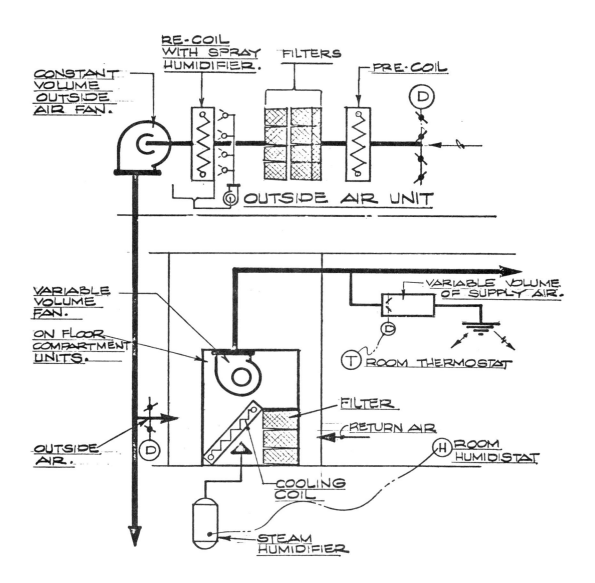

RE·COIL
WITH SPRAY
HUMIDIFIER.

FILTERS

PRE·COIL

CONSTANT
VOLUME
OUTSIDE
AIR FAN.

D

OUTSIDE AIR UNIT

VARIABLE
VOLUME
FAN.

ON FLOOR
COMPARTMENT
UNITS.

VARIABLE VOLUME
OF SUPPLY AIR.

D

T ROOM THERMOSTAT

FILTER

RETURN AIR

H ROOM
HUMIDISTAT

OUTSIDE
AIR.

D

COOLING
COIL

STEAM
HUMIDIFIER

Figure 7:   Combination of outside ventilation unit
and floor-mounted compartment unit.

cools and partially dehumidifies the outside air before it is delivered to the on-floor compartment unit. The amount of air supplied is fixed at the minimum required for occupant ventilation and the system only operates during occupied hours.

Recirculation type on-floor compartment units provide cooling, dehumidification, and humidification to the floor zone. Air is controlled at a constant temperature off the unit cooling coil and is distributed through medium and low pressure ductwork to variable air terminals and linear troffer diffusers.

To maintain constant dry bulb conditions the variable air terminal varies the mass of air supply to suit the changing cooling load. If the partial humidification provided by the outside air spray coil humidifier is insufficient to maintain desired floor zone humidity, then the on-floor electrode clean steam humidifier adds the additional moisture required. High humidities are limited by the maximum dewpoint off the on-floor unit cooling coil.

The specific methods of air and water control are shown on figures 8 and 9.

From these it can be seen that the water loop reclaims heat from the on-floor units to heat the outside air and provide adiabatic humidification.

Additionally it is obvious that the absolute humidity provided from an on-floor unit is the same for the entire zone, whilst the dry bulb may be separately controlled throughout the zone.

The advantages of this approach are:

- minimum use of outside air, hence limited introduction of gaseous and particulate contaminants plus reduced winter humidification energy requirements.

- limited effect on environmental conditions if a conditioning unit fails, particularly humidity.

- flexible floor-by-floor variations in humidity (even if only nominal).

- reduced fan energy requirements resulting from shorter on-floor duct runs and air mass flow variations.

Figure 8: Outside air vent unit to on-floor unit control.

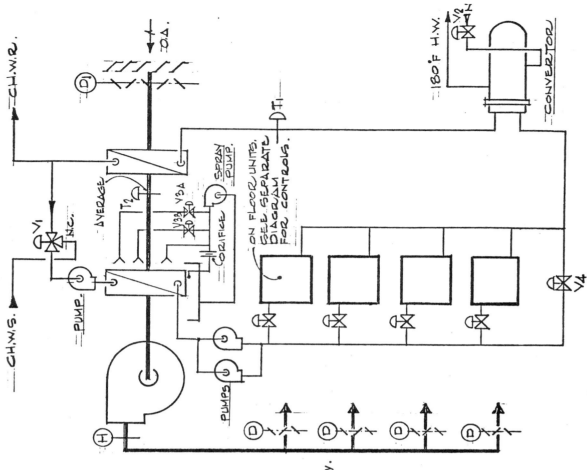

Sequence of Operation:

Occupied:

Outside air unit on, controls energized.

D1 fully open.
T1 modulates V1 to obtain set value (≈62°F).
If measured value T1 falls by ≈20F (60°F) T1 modulates V2 to maintain 60°F.
T2 overrides T1 when temperature falls to 40°F, closes V1 and modulates V2
  to obtain minimum 40°F - freeze stat set at 35°F.

Pressure differential sensor P modulates V4 to maintain minimum 80% design
flow of pump.

Dew point sensor H cycles valves V3A, V3B, to obtain dew point between
32/35°F.

Dampers D to on-floor units to open as directed by on-floor unit control.

Smoke sensor and high temperature fire sensor to stop O.A. unit on emergency.
These controls to be manual reset.

Unoccupied:

Outside air unit off, D1 closed.
Humidity controls off.
Controls to V1, V2, T1, T2, V4 and P energized.
Secondary pumps energized.

Figure 9: On-floor unit control.

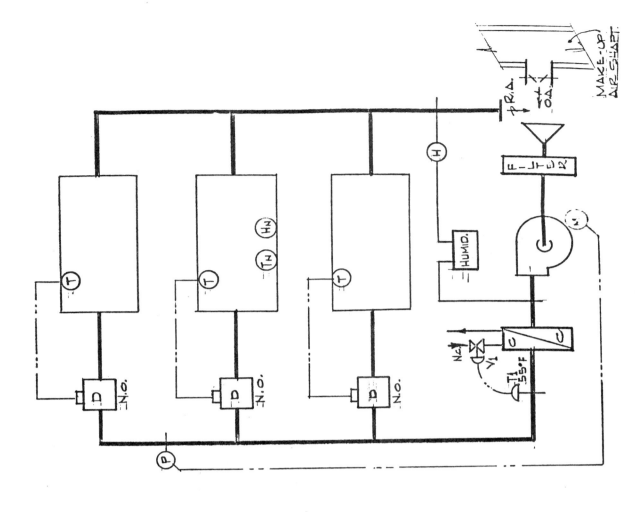

Sequence of Operation:

Day (Occupied):

Controls energized except T_N, H_N.
O.A. damper open.
T_1 modulates V_1 to obtain set value - 56°F.
P modulates motor M to obtain set value - 0.25" w.g..
H modulates humidifier heat input to obtain 25/35/50% R.H.
T modulates V.A.V. box D to obtain 74°F.

When fire alarm system indicates a fire condition on the floor,
damper D closes and unit stops.

Night (Unoccupied):   - Fan and Controls Off

H_N measures specific room condition, if humidity drops below set
value approximately 3/4% below return air. Humidity set point
starts fan and energizes humidifier.
O.A. damper closed.
V.A.V. boxes full open (R.A.)
C.C. control closed.

T_N measures specific room temperature if temperature rises above
set value (say 78°F). Fan is energized, cooling coil control is
energized, V.A.V. boxes energized.

When both H_N and T_N satisfied in night mode, fan stops and through
cycling relay does not restart for set time, say 15 minutes.

- opportunity to turn off conditioning to a floor when
  not required without affecting other floors which
  may be critical. (In this regard it is perhaps worth
  noting that both in California and New York, museums
  have found that in a building with little or no in-
  filtration, air-conditioning units can be turned off
  at night without marked effect on the maintained
  conditions.)

- greater safety, since in the event of a fire on a
  floor, smoke would only be recirculated on that floor.

For efficient energy utilization, the heat of lights, equipment, people, and, when available, solar energy will be reclaimed by the air systems to heat the building and domestic
hot water. Unconditioned, outside dilution air for fume
hoods and canopies will be introduced at the hood or canopy
to reduce thermal penalties imposed on the room environment.
Occupied space load will be reduced by using on-floor fans,
eliminating the need to operate a central system when only
one space on one floor need be conditioned. In addition,
fan energy will be reduced by varying the mass of air supplied by the system to meet the occupied space load.

B. Performance Specifications for Micro-Climate Units

William Maxwell, Jr., M.E. and Stephen Stone, M.E.

1.0   GENERAL

This specification describes the performance criteria
for a family of temperature and relative humidity conditioning equipment. These units are to be used with
moderately well-sealed exhibition cases in three size
ranges. The units will be designed to fit within a
space below the exhibition case, will be capable of
being powered by standard electrical inputs and will
interface with the case in an unobtrusive manner.

1.1   Scope

This specification is intended as a means of defining
the required micro-climate end products necessary for
the conservation of certain objects. These end results are capable of being produced by a variety of
mechanical, electrical and chemical techniques. The
specification makes no attempt to fix those techniques
applicable to each micro-climatizer.

1.2   Classification

The units shall be classified into two types and will
be provided in three size configurations.

1.2.1 Type A Humidifier

Units in this category shall be capable of increasing
the relative humidity (RH) within the conditioned
space. They shall also have the ability to heat or
cool air to maintain a fixed temperature-humidity
condition.

1.2.2 Type B Dehumidifier

Units in this category shall be capable of decreasing the RH within the conditioned space. They shall also have the ability to heat or cool air to maintain a fixed temperature-humidity condition.

1.2.3 Type C Dehumidifier

Units in this category shall be capable of decreasing the RH within the conditioned space. They shall also have the ability to heat or cool air to maintain a fixed temperature-humidity condition.

1.2.4 Load Range Type A or B Units

A1 - Humidifier for space of 10 to 50 cubic feet.

A2 - Humidifier for space of 100 to 200 cubic feet.

A3 - Humidifier for space of 400 to 1,000 cubic feet.

B1 - Dehumidifier for space of 10 to 50 cubic feet.

B2 - Dehumidifier for space of 100 to 200 cubic feet.

B3 - Dehumidifier for space of 400 to 1,000 cubic feet.

For load ranges falling between the specified units (such as 80 cubic feet) the nearest load range unit up in size from the required unit shall apply.

2.0 APPLICABLE SPECIFICATIONS

Equipment to be supplied shall meet applicable portions of Underwriters Laboratories (U.L.) and/or Canadian Standards Association (C.S.A.) requirements and shall comply with national and regional electrical code requirements.

3.0 OUTPUT CHARACTERISTICS

3.1 Relative Humidity

All type A units (humidifiers) shall be capable of producing a constant RH within the conditioned space of 50± 2%. This output shall be maintained within the full range of all input conditions.

All type B units (dehumidifiers) shall be capable of producing a constant RH within the conditioned space of 20± 2%. This output shall be maintained within the full range of all input conditions.

3.2.1 Temperature, Type A or B Units

Both type A and B units of all sizes shall be capable of maintaining the conditioned space at a temperature between 21° and 23.5°C (70 and 76°F ± 2°F).

3.2.2 Temperature, Type C Units

Type C units shall be capable of maintaining the conditioned space at a temperature of 4°C + 1° (40°F + 2°).

3.3 Make-up Air

Units of all types will supply air in quantities shown herein (see para. 3.3.1) in order to make up for air leakage from the cases. This make-up air shall be re-filtered for particulate matter to a level of 99% efficiency to 10 microns and 90 to 95% efficiency to 1 micron and for sulphur dioxide, ozone, and nitrous oxide by the use of charcoal or equivalent filtration.

3.3.1 Airflow Rates

Type A1 and B1 units shall have the capability of supplying a minimum of 2.0 cubic feet per hour (CFH).

Type A2 and B2 units shall have the capability of supplying a minimum of 8.5 CFH.

Type A3 and B3 units shall have the capability of supplying a minimum of 45 CFH.

3.4 Cooling and/or Heating Capacity

Units shall have the capability of modifying the case interior temperature to within the limits specified in paragraph 3.2. The units shall be capable of cooling and/or heating the supply air to achieve this result. Heating or cooling loads will be dependent upon the process used for humidity control and for case surface heat load. A case surface heat load of 7 watts per square foot, from lighting, shall be used for computations. Affected surface area for A1 and B1 units shall be considered to be 25 square feet; for A2 and B2 units the area shall be considered to be 50 square feet; for A3 and B3 units the area shall be considered to be 125 square feet.

3.5 Sound Level

The equipment for the micro-climate units shall operate at a sound level not exceeding NC-35 of the noise criteria curves recommended by the American Society of Heating, Refrigerating and Air Conditioning Engineers. This criterion may be exceeded during hours when the Museum is not open to the public if significant savings in efficiency, ease of operation, or cost can be realized.

3.6 Vibration

The equipment for the micro-climate units shall be designed and isolated such that the transmitted vibration from the equipment to the exhibition case and the exhibits shall be negligible.

4.0 INPUT CHARACTERISTICS

All micro-climate units will be subject to the following conditions:

4.1 Environmental Conditions

4.1.1 Temperature and Humidity

Air temperature surrounding the exterior of the exhibition cases and air available for make-up shall be provided at a temperature between 21° and 23.5°C (70° and 76°F $\pm$ 2°) and at relative humidities ranging from 25% to 50% $\pm$ 10%.

4.1.2 Air Quality

The surrounding ambient (building) air shall have been filtered for particulate matter to 99% to 10 microns and 90% to 95% to 1 micron. It shall also have been passed through a charcoal or equivalent filter to remove SO_2, O_3, and NO_x.

4.1.3 Electrical

Each unit shall be capable of operation when supplied with electrical power with the following characteristics: 120 volts A.C., 1 phase, 60 Hz, 15 amperes.

4.1.4 <u>Other</u>

Specific designs may require input water lines, drains
or exhaust ports. Each of these, if required, shall
be co-ordinated with the proper Museum personnel for
size, location, and availability.

5.0 <u>PHYSICAL CONSIDERATIONS</u>

5.1 <u>Size and Weight</u>

The equipment to be utilized in the micro-climate con-
trollers shall fit within a space to be provided below the exhibition case and shall not exceed 4 cubic
feet in volume for size 1 and 2 units, and 8 cubic
feet in volume for size 3 units, exclusive of storage
containers (such as water tanks) which may be required.
Available space for storage containers shall be identified by and co-ordinated with Museum personnel where
such containers are necessary for a specific design.
Wherever possible designs should limit equipment
weight such that installation and removal may be easily accomplished without the need for special lifting
or handling equipment.

5.2 <u>Materials and Workmanship</u>

Materials selected for use in the units shall be such
that they do not introduce contaminants into the micro-
climate. Materials shall also be selected for minimal
maintenance and long life. Workmanship shall be provided on a level to best commercial quality.

6.0 <u>LIFE, RELIABILITY, AND MAINTAINABILITY</u>

Each micro-climate unit shall be designed and constructed such that it will be capable of 24-hour-per-day,
365-day-per-year operation with a minimum of repairs,
replacements, or downtime. A design goal for equipment
life should be such that a minimum of five years of
operation can be attained without major overhaul or re-
placement of major components. Redundant components
may be used if necessary to achieve the required life
and to provide reliable, trouble-free equipment.

Ease of maintenance must be considered when designing
the units. Access doors, plug-in modules, quick

connect circuits, and similar techniques for improving maintainability shall be provided wherever applicable.

7.0   <u>EQUIPMENT INTERFACE</u>

Each micro-climate unit shall be designed to interface with a particular exhibition case. Inlet and return air openings to the case input electrical power lines, water inlets and drains, openings for ambient air inlet and return shall all be designed for compatability between case and micro-climate unit. Type A and B units of a particular size must be interchangeable with respect to interface so that an exhibition case may be utilized for many types of object.

8.0   <u>INSTRUMENTATION AND CONTROLS</u>

8.1   <u>Controls</u>

Each unit shall have, as a minimum, a switch for energizing the equipment, a light indicating that the equipment has been energized, and a setting for the control of relative humidity. Humidifiers (type A) shall be adjustable from 30% to 70% RH. Dehumidifiers shall be adjustable from 5% to 40% RH. Controls shall be easily accessible to operating personnel but shall be protected from inadvertent disturbance.

8.2   <u>Instrumentation</u>

Each micro-climate unit shall be provided with a signal device such as an indicating light which will signal an out-of-tolerance condition. This light shall be visible on the exterior of the exhibition case so that a guard or personnel assigned to micro-climate checking may see the signal readily. In addition, the specific out-of-tolerance condition, (i.e., high humidity, low humidity, high temperature) shall be indicated on the equipment control panel and shall be visible when the unit is checked at the exhibition case. In addition the units shall be equipped with plug-in read-out ports such that the actual RH and temperature may be indicated or recorded near the exhibition case by plugging in a specific indicator or recorder for relative humidity or temperature. The selection of type of instrumentation shall be co-ordinated with cognizant Museum personnel. The intention is to have each micro-climate controlled case equipped with the ability for read-out (sensors) and to have several portable read-out devices, both indicating and recording types, which will be utilized on specific cases as deemed necessary.

Annotated Bibliography

This bibliography was included in the advance information package sent to workshop participants. It was compiled as a survey of literature on existing micro-climate solutions. Representative contributions in each area were selected and the entries were annotated to provide participants with an immediate reference document.

Abbreviations

AAM   American Association of Museums

AATA   Art and Archaeology Technical Abstracts (published
                                              by the IIC)

CCI   Canadian Conservation Institute

CMA   Canadian Museums Association

ICOM   International Council of Museums

IIC   International Institute for the Conservation of
         Historic and Artistic Works

IIC-CG   International Institute for the Conservation of
         Historic and Artistic Works - Canadian Group

1. RELATIVE HUMIDITY AND TEMPERATURE CONTROL

a) PHYSICAL BARRIERS OR ENCLOSURES

Gallery Size

Amdur, E.J.

"Humidity Control - Isolated Area Plan", Museum News, 43:4, Technical Supplement No. 6 (December 1964), pp. 58-60

Amdur, chief engineer for Honeywell Inc. in 1965, describes a "building within a building" approach to humidification in cold climates.

Toishi, Kenzo;
Kenjo, Toshiko;
Ishikawa, Rikuo

"About Temperature and Humidity within Exhibit Galleries and Repositories", Science for Conservation, 8 (1972), pp. 7-24 (AATA 9-478)

A comparison of adiabatic (impassable to heat) properties of various wall boards for interior coverings of galleries.

Thomson, Garry

"Impermanence: Some Chemical and Physical Aspects", Museums Journal, 64:1, (1964), pp. 16-36 (AATA 5-5103)

Chemical change in the museum
- energy of activation
- heat energy
- light energy
- extent of damage

Movement of water in organic material
- the closed container at constant temperature
- the closed container in a varying temperature
- temporary container for the Leonardo cartoon
- closed cases and packaging for transport

Technical section
- temperature and rate of deterioration
- use of inert gases for the protection of museum objects
- the chemistry of embrittlement
- movement and failure

Showcase Size

Diamond, Michael   "A Micro-micro-climate", <u>Museums Journal</u>,
                   73:4 (March 1974), pp. 161-163
                   (AATA 11-442)

                   A box of hardwood with a chipboard back
                   and rubber gasket, the interior lined
                   with blue-grey velvet and fitted with
                   panels containing silica gel and a small
                   Edney 2" dial hygrometer.

Hillen, John   "Modular Exhibit System", CMA <u>Gazette</u>,
                   10:2, (Spring 1977), pp. 6-10

                   A modular case system in two sizes - 57"
                   x 60" x 8" deep (at narrowest) and 29" x
                   61" x 22" deep (at narrowest), equipped
                   with UV control, heat control, dust-
                   proofing, moisture control (silica gel),
                   and security control.

Padfield, Tim   "Design of Museum Showcases", <u>London Con-
                   ference on Museum Climatology</u> (IIC: Lon-
                   don, rev. ed. 1968), p. 119

                   Padfield deals with the permeability of
                   plastic materials and the difficulty of
                   maintaining a controlled environment in
                   glazed cases; he recommends absorbent
                   materials in cases. He discusses ventil-
                   ation holes and dust and pollution fil-
                   ters such as activated carbon (500 g/m^3
                   of case). Protection from internally
                   generated acid pollutants is suggested
                   using cloth impregnated with magnesium
                   carbonate. Included are drawings of some
                   ways of sealing glass to metal.

Stolow, Nathan   "Fundamental Case Design for Humidity
                   Sensitive Museum Collections", <u>Museum
                   News</u>, 44:6, Technical Supplement No. 11
                   (February 1966)

                   An early technical report on testing of
                   various absorbent case materials and
                   buffering agents for use in a sealed case.

Stolow, Nathan   "The Micro-climate: a Localized Solution",
  (cont'd)   <u>Museum News</u> 56:2 (November/December 1977),
   pp. 52-63

A review of the need for micro-climates
and discussion of:
1. the effect of temperature change on
   RH and the relationship between case
   volume and object size during these
   changes;
2. factors which encourage "breathing"
   of a case;
3. buffers (silica gel, Nikka pellets,
   etc.).

Thomson, Garry   "Stabilization of Relative Humidity in
Exhibition Cases: Hygrometric Half-time",
<u>Studies in Conservation</u>, 22:2 (May 1977),
p. 85

A formula is derived with experimental
support for predicting the RH changes inside a case containing a buffer such as
silica gel. The case should be non-permeable and is described; 20 kg of silica
gel is required per cubic metre.

Condon, Edward   "Preservation of the Declaration of Independence and the Constitution of the
United States", Washington [U.S. Govern-
ment Printing Office] National Bureau of
Standards, Circular 505, (1951)

The Declaration of Independence has been
enclosed in an hermetically sealed case
filled with helium. Included in the case
was a quantity of cellulosic materials
of known moisture content which acted as
a buffer for any internal RH changes resulting from room temperature variations.

b) <u>BUFFERS</u>

American Society   "Dehumidification by Sorbent Materials",
of Heating,   <u>Guide and Data Book, 1962: Applications</u>,
Refrigerating   p. 853
and Air-condi-
tioning Engineers
(ASHRE)

Boustead, W.M.

"Dehumidification in Museum Storage Areas", <u>London Conference on Museum Climatology</u> (IIC: London, Rev. ed. 1968), pp. 103-107

- humidity control by refrigeration
- humidity control by lithium chloride
- adsorbents vs. absorbents
- areas of application for portable lithium chloride units.

Putti, G. and Faggion, S.

"Painting for Temperature Control", <u>Pitture Vernici</u>, 50:9 (1974), pp. 327-331 (AATA 12-715)

The effect of external paint on the temperature reached by buildings, containers, etc. on exposure to solar radiation is considered. Differences resulting from the use of white or black paint or metallic surfaces are indicated.

Toishi, Kenzo and Miura, Sadatoshi

"Purification of Air with Zeolite", <u>Science for Conservation</u>, 14 (March 1977), pp. 1-7 (AATA 12-1052)

The Mona Lisa was exhibited for 50 days in the Tokyo National Museum in spring, 1974, in a closed iron case lined with a 75 mm glass layer and double panel glass window. Zeolite was used to maintain 50% RH.

Noonan, Carl

"Solving a Humidity Control Problem", CMA <u>Gazette</u>, 8:2 (Spring 1975), pp. 21-25 (AATA 12-677)

Construction of a sealed display cabinet for a wood panel, incorporating a fan, silica gel, and fittings to maintain 66% RH.

Organ, R.M.

"The Safe Storage of Unstable Glass", <u>Museums Journal</u>, 56:11 (February 1957), pp. 265-272

Organ, R.M.
  (cont'd)

A method for keeping "sweating" glass below 42% RH. This figure represents the proportion of possible moisture in the atmosphere when potassium carbonate (a product of glass breakdown) is wet. Two wood and glass cases of 80 cu. ft. each were used, with an axial-flow fan circulating air downward over silica gel. Case details and a sketch are included.

Padfield, Tim

"The Control of Relative Humidity and Air Pollution in Show Cases and Picture Frames", Studies in Conservation 11:1 (1966), pp. 8-30 (AATA 6-A5-37)

- absorbent materials and their use
- exchange processes between case and outside
- air flow caused by temperature and pressure changes
- air flow by convection

Padfield suggests a method of reducing exchange by controlling air flow and RH control by sodium bromide under a silicone rubber membrane.

Sack, Susanne P.

"A Case Study of Humidity Control", Brooklyn Museum Annual 5 (1963-64), pp. 99-103 (AATA 5-5097)

Describes a controlled environment made for a panel painting during winter RH of 12 to 28% in 1963. A large sealed wooden case with a double glass door held pans containing a saturated solution of magnesium nitrate hexahydrate and a small fan. The RH was held at 50% to 52%.

Toishi, Kenzo

"Humidity Control in a Closed Package", Studies in Conservation, 4 (1959), pp. 81-87

Discusses characteristics of various substances with reference to humidity. A table of percentage expansion of various seasoned woods is included. Mention is made of silica gel and Kaken gel, which is made from active clay particles coated with a form of silica gel.

Wood as a Buffer

Barrer, R.M.

Diffusion in and Through Solids, (Cambridge University Press, 1941)

Martin, Kurt

"Extension of the Exhibition Rooms at the Alte Pinakothek, Munich", Museum, 15 (1962), pp. 146-151 (Paris: UNESCO), (AATA 5-5093)

Wood parquetry floors and wood-panelled or fabric walls are used for buffering.

Stamm, A.J.

"Passage of Liquids, Vapours and Dissolved Materials Through Soft Woods", U.S. Department of Agriculture Technical Bulletin, 929 (1946)

Thomson, Garry

"Relative Humidity - Variation with Temperature in a Case Containing Wood", Studies in Conservation, 9 (1964) pp. 153-169 (AATA 5-5104)

Experiments proving that in a closed case with quantities of wood in excess of about 100 g/100 l of air, the change in RH will not exceed about 1/3 of the temperature change, and will be in the same direction, provided there is no entry of outside air into the case.

Toishi, Kenzo et al.

"Difference of Wood Materials as Buffers Against Changes of Atmospheric Humidity", Science for Conservation, 6 (March 1970), pp. 25-36 (AATA 8-729)

A study of the equilibrium moisture content of various woods under different temperatures and RH. There is a general tendency that lighter wood has a larger capacity of moisture content, and under change of temperature in an airtight space, displays a greater speed of moisture absorption and discharge.

c) MECHANICAL SOLUTIONS

Consumer Reports   "Dehumidifiers", <u>Consumer Reports</u>, 39:8 (August 1974), pp. 618-622 (AATA 11-434)

Boustead, W.M.   "Dehumidification in Museum Storage Areas", <u>London Conference on Museum Climatology</u>, (IIC: London, rev. ed. 1968), pp. 103-107

Use of the heat pump.

Convectron Inc.   "ACE - Art in a Controlled Environment" (Washington, D.C.: National Endowment for the Arts, 1971; not published)

Research, design, and prototype of a "space capsule" for the shipping and viewing of paintings in a 100 cu. ft. environment, controlled for shock, vibration, humidity, temperature, light, particulate matter, intrusion, security, and fire (thermoelectric and vapour cycle).

Organ, R.M.   "Humidification of Galleries for a Temporary Exhibition", <u>London Conference on Museum Climatology</u>, (IIC: London, rev. ed. 1968), pp. 1-13

For the ROM Japanese Art Treasures exhibition, 1965. Organ describes modifications to an existing air-conditioning system to provide for temporary circulation to an additional, non-conditioned area, by a combination of:
1. dampering the re-circualtion duct;
2. installation of a steam valve and pierced 2 cm copper pipe to serve as a steam-jet humidifier;
3. atomizer units with automatic filling mechanisms. Some practical disadvantages of aerosol humidifiers are noted.

2. DUST AND POLLUTANT CONTROL

Garver, Thomas H.

"Control of Atmospheric Pollutants and Maintenance of Stable Climatic Conditions", London Conference on Museum Climatology, (IIC: London, rev. ed. 1968), pp. 22-35

A review of four general types of air cleaning devices:
1. air washers or scrubbers
2. mechanical air filters which trap particulate matter by impingement with viscous surfaces or within fibrous mats
3. electronic air cleaners
4. adsorptive materials such as activated charcoal.

Kadokura, Takeo

"A Study on the Dust in the Air Surrounding Cultural Properties", Science for Conservation, 14 (March 1975), pp. 17-25 (AATA 12-673)

An investigation of the dust in depositories, exhibition rooms, and showcases of the Nara National Museum was carried out by using a particle counter, Climate Controlled Environmental Monitor model C1-250. The air sent into the depositories had been sufficiently cleaned by air-conditioners; the concentration of dust in them was 1/10 to about 1/100 of that of the air outside. When a party of 400 visitors stayed in the exhibition the concentration of dust in it increased 10 times, but dropped to one third in 15 to 20 minutes after the party left.

Kenjo, Toshiko and Toishi, Kenzo

"Purification of Air with Zeolite", Science for Conservation, 12 (March 1975), pp. 27-31 (AATA 12-674)

Zeolite was found to be capable of adsorbing various gases such as sulphur dioxide, hydrogen sulphide, ammonia, gaso-

Kenjo, Toshiko and Toishi, Kenzo

(cont'd)

line vapour, carbon dioxide, and formaldehyde. The zeolite had been brought to humidity equilibrium in air at RH 60%; the amounts of various gases adsorbed on it were measured.

Krogh, A.

"The Dust Problem in Museums and How to Solve It", Museums Journal, 47:10 (1948), pp. 183-188

Discusses various causes of temperature and pressure variations which bring dust into cases, and suggests the use of small case holes which contain filters. A number of filtering materials are discussed, with the exact size of holes in relation to the volume of air in the case. The article contains a section on the protection of insect drawers and small showcases.

Organ, R.M.

"Remarks on Inhibitors Used in Steam Humidification", IIC-AG Bulletin, 7:2 (1967), p. 31

The effect of volatile amines on copper compounds.

Toishi, Kenzo and Kenjo, Toshiko

"Some Aspects of the Conservation of Art in Buildings of New Concrete", Studies in Conservation, 20:2 (May 1975), pp. 118-122 (AATA 12-1191)

Part I discusses the properties of concrete, aerosols liberated from concrete, and the precise effects of alkaline air on linseed oil, silk, some pigments, and hair hygrometers. It suggests some methods tried to counteract the effects of new concrete, the most successful of which was a high temperature seasoning time of "a summer or two".
Part II describes a simple method of measuring the alkalinity of air in new concrete buildings.

Toishi, Kenzo and Sekino, M.

"The Fine Arts Museum at Expo '70, Osaka: Conservation Techniques", <u>Museum</u>, 24:2 (1972), pp. 66-68 (Paris: UNESCO) (AATA 11-63)

Describes the 17-unit air-conditioning system. An attempt was made to control RH at 55%± 5%, with some Oriental objects kept in an atmosphere of 60%± 5%. There were many admirable features of the building design; the main defects were the chimney effect of the high building design, inadequate control of lighting, and marble floors which created lime dust. The building was too new and needed time to reach the environmental equilibrium needed for museum purposes.

3. LIGHT/HEAT CONTROL

Ellard, P.

"Museum Lighting", Appendix I of <u>Communicating with the Museum Visitor - Guidelines for Planning</u>, (Toronto: ROM, 1971)

Feller, Robert L.

"Control of Deteriorating Effects of Light upon Museum Objects: Heating Effects of Illuminating by Incandescent Lamps", <u>Museum News</u>, 46, Technical Supplement (May 1968)

Hanlan, J.F.

"Museum Lighting Control: An Annotated Bibliography", paper given at the Ontario Museum Association seminar on lighting, November 1977

Hardy, A.C. and O'Sullivan, P.E.

Insulation and Fenestration (Newcastle-upon-Tyne, Oriel Press Limited, 1967)

An investigation into the problems of overheating in multi-storey buildings, as a result of solar radiation through large glass areas.

Harris, J.B.   "Practical Aspects of Lighting as Relat-
                            ed to Conservation", London Conference
                            on Museum Climatology, (IIC: London, rev.
                            ed. 1968), G. Thomson, ed. pp. 133-138

Harrison,   Report on the Deteriorating Effects of
    Laurence S.   Modern Light Sources, (New York: Metro-
                            politan Museum of Modern Art, 1954)

                            "Evaluation of Spectral Radiation Haz-
                            ards in Window Lighted Galleries", IIC
                            Recent Advances in Conservation, (London:
                            Butterworth, 1963), pp. 1-6

Illuminating   "Museums and Art Galleries", IES Light-
Engineering   ing Handbook, 5th ed. (1972), sec. 12:18-
Society (IES)   12:25

Kallstrom, O. and   "Lighting Methods for Showcases; Exhibi-
Olson, G.   tion and Research Work at the Statens
                            Historiska Museum, Stockholm", Museum
                            4:3 (1951), pp. 201-211 (Paris: UNESCO)

Lafontaine,   Comparison of the Efficiency of Ultra-
    Raymond   violet Absorbing Compounds, (Ottawa:
                            Canadian Conservation Institute, 1974)

Kuehn, Hermann   "The Effect of Oxygen, Relative Humidity
                            and Temperature on the Fading Rate of
                            Watercolours. Reduced Light Damage in a
                            Nitrogen Atmosphere." London Conference
                            on Museum Climatology (IIC: London, rev.
                            ed. 1968), pp. 79-88

Macleod, K.J.   "Museum Lighting", CCI Technical
                            Bulletin, 2 (April 1975)

Padfield, Tim and   "The Light Fastness of the Natural Dyes",
Landi, S.   Studies in Conservation, 11:4 (1966),
                            pp. 181-196

Thomson, Garry

"A New Look at Colour Rendering, Level of Illumination and Protection from Ultraviolet Radiation in Museum Lighting", <u>Studies in Conservation</u>, 6:2-3 (1961)

<u>Conservation and Museum Lighting</u>, (London: Museum Association, 2nd ed. 1974)

4. <u>GENERAL ENVIRONMENT</u>

Matthai, Robert H. (ed.)

<u>Protection of Collections During Energy Emergencies</u>, AAM, March 1978

Brommelle, N.S.

"Technical Services – Air Conditioning and Lighting from the Point of View of Conservation", <u>Museums Journal</u>, 63:1-2 (1965), pp. 32-36 (AATA 6-A5-6)

Buck, Richard D. and Amdur, Elias J.

"A Specification for Museum Air-conditioning and Humidity Control", <u>Museum News</u>, 43, Technical Supplement 5 (December 1964)

Has a humidity tolerance table.

Buck, Richard D.

"On Conservation: How Does the Energy Crisis Affect the Conservation of Museum Collections?", <u>Museum News</u>, 52:7 (April 1974), pp. 8-9 (AATA 11-470)

Convectron Inc.

"Preparation of Historic Sites for Public Use", Project prepared for the State of New York Parks and Recreation Department on 12 historic sites, 1976 to the present.

Design and working drawings of environmental and security systems for historic buildings housing furniture and fine arts collections.

Douglas, R. Alan   "A Commonsense Approach to Environmental Control", <u>Curator</u>, 15:2 (June 1972), pp. 139-144

Engineering Interface   Report on Environmental Requirements of ROM Collections and Possible Means of Achieving Proper Conditions (November 1976)

MacLeod, K.J.   "Relative Humidity: Its Importance, Measurement and Control in Museums", <u>CCI Technical Bulletin No. 1</u> (April 1975)

McGuiness, John J.   "Environmental Control for Historic Properties: The Important Role of Humidity Regulation", <u>Technology and Conservation of Art, Architecture and Antiquities</u> 1:3 (1976), pp. 22-32 (AATA 14-37)

National Research Council   <u>Abstracts: Environmental Effects on Materials and Equipment</u> (Prevention of Deterioration Centre)

Plenderleith, H.J. and Werner, A.E.A.   <u>The Conservation of Antiquities and Works of Art: Treatment, Repair and Restoration</u>, (London, 1971)

Plenderleith, H.J. and Philippot, P.   "Climatology and Conservation in Museums", <u>Museum</u>, 12:4 (1960), pp. 201-289 (Paris: UNESCO)

Rogers, George de W.   "The Ideal of the Ideal Environment", <u>Journal of IIC-CG</u>, 2:1 (Autumn 1976), p. 34

"The Environment and Collections", <u>CCI Newsletter</u>, 4 (August 1974); 5 (November 1974) (AATA 13-184)

Stolow, Nathan   "Conservation of Works of Art and Exhib-
                        tions", paper presented at ICOM
                        Leningrad Conference (May 1977)

Thomson, Garry   "Planning the Preservation of Our
                        Cultural Heritage", Museum, 25:1-2 (1973),
                        pp. 15-25 (Paris: UNESCO) (AATA 11-459)